PROFESSIONAL PILOT

Professional
Pilot

JOHN LOWERY

IOWA STATE UNIVERSITY PRESS • AMES

THIS BOOK IS DEDICATED TO

Colonel Antoinette T. Lowery, USAF (NC),

who in her own right has over 1000 hours as medical
crew director in the Air Force C-9 Nightingale: the most
competent, professional, and attractive colonel I've
ever known—my wife.

John Lowery is an aviation consultant and training specialist. He flew for Western and Frontier
Airlines in the middle 1950s and subsequently spent 23 years in the United States Air Force flying
and testing high performance aircraft.

©1983 The Iowa State University Press. All rights reserved. Composed and printed by The Iowa State University
Press, Ames, Iowa 50010

First edition, 1983

Library of Congress Cataloging in Publication Data

Lowery, John.
  Professional pilot.

  1. Aeronautics–Safety measures. 2. Airplanes–Piloting. I. Title.
TL553.5.L69   1983   629.132′52   82–17207
ISBN 0-8138-1411-1

CONTENTS

WHEN serious pilots begin to look beyond the aircraft systems training they have received at most flight schools, they are immediately stopped by the lack of ready references. Because of this problem certain important aerodynamic facts are not readily available except perhaps by hearsay. Yet the National Aeronautics and Space Administration, the United States Navy, the United States Air Force, and manufacturers have a wealth of facts that pilots of sophisticated aircraft need to know. Two classic reference sources are *Aerodynamics for Naval Aviators* by H. H. Hurt of the University of Southern California and "Aerodynamics for Pilots," Air Training Command Manual 51-3. Others are listed in the Bibliography.

This book contains flying techniques, rules of thumb, and facts of flight gleaned from the various reference sources and from my own 30 years as a professional pilot. National Transportation Safety Board 5 year average accident statistics reflect a consistent pattern that varies little from year to year. Roughly 20% of accidents occur during takeoff and 42% during landing. Takeoff and landing are sometimes referred to as the critical 8 min of flight; 2 min during takeoff and 6 min during approach and landing. Another 34% of accidents occur during in-flight operations; they account for 68% of general aviation fatalities.

This book has been written with these facts in mind. Each chapter discusses in depth the aerodynamic principles involved in a particular phase of flight that has had recurring accidents. For example, Federal Aviation Regulations takeoff limitations for light twins are not as clearly defined as for transport category airplanes. Therefore the light twin pilot must understand thoroughly the manufacturer's performance charts and when and how to use accelerate-stop, accelerate-go, and normal takeoff distance figures. FARs 91, 135, and 121 carefully spell out to pilots of transport category airplanes (those grossing over 12,500 lb and all turbojets) specific runway limitations for takeoff and weight limitations for climb after loss of the critical engine.

High Mach flight is extremely important to pilots of jet aircraft. Yet the nonmilitary trained pilot has no ready reference source from which to learn. Ignorance of the forces involved has led a number of pilots to disable the Mach warning system by pulling the circuit breaker or switching off an illegal on-off switch. This act is thought to have led to several recent accidents in which the aircraft impacted at a steep dive angle at great speed.

Because of fuel costs, cruise control is especially important for pilots of both propeller and turbojet aircraft. Mishaps due to fuel exhaustion indicate a

PREFACE

possible lack of knowledge or a lack of thorough training in the finer points involved. Each type of aircraft—reciprocating, turboprop, or jet—requires specific procedures to be followed if economy and safety are not to be compromised. The stall/spin factor has been a persistent problem; yet little usable information is available on the subject. This topic is thoroughly covered in Chapters 9 and 10.

Considerable detail concerning the landing phase of flight is neglected in many training programs, and it is not found in the various airplane flight manuals. Chapters 11–15 deal in depth with several aspects that have led to accidents.

And finally, there is the very hostile high altitude environment in which pilots of pressurized airplanes work. While no FAR requires a pilot to be trained in high altitude effects, a sudden decompression places both pilots and passengers in a life or death situation with only seconds to accomplish lifesaving procedures. Information on this subject is included, but only the hands-on training available in the Federal Aviation Administration Oklahoma City high altitude chamber or one of the military physiological training facilities really qualifies a pilot to cope with high altitude emergencies.

Special thanks are due Frank Quinn of Executive Air Fleet (Teterboro); Jack L. Isaac (Seattle), Western Airlines (retired); Allen Schwab, Pan American Airlines; and FAA test pilot, Tom Wright for their editorial help and critical comments. To Murray Smith, publisher of *Professional Pilot* magazine, I am forever appreciative for the opportunity to help spread the message that safety, knowledge, and professionalism are integral to all flying operations.

Every year more than 80% of general aviation aircraft accidents are attributed to pilot error. Failure of an aircraft system that results in an accident is rare. Rather, lack of attention to aircraft performance and poor pilot technique and judgment are the primary causes. Much of this pilot error, I feel, is a training deficiency because so much information and so many important piloting techniques are omitted from flight manuals and professional training programs.

I hope this book will be a source of information for serious pilots that will help them make sound decisions when conditions are less than optimum. Above all, remember, that as the captain of an aircraft, safety is your primary consideration. The accidents don't always happen to the other guy.

John Lowery

Earthly encumbered; living to fly;
Taking to wing; coming alive.

Abode in blue; furnished in white;
Carpet in terra; effortless flight.

Gliding on sunlight; highways of air;
Hum to the winds' song; little to care.

Soar above eagles; the zephyr a foe;
Chasing the evening; miles quickly flow.

Talons are readied; sleekness at cost;
Once more ungainly; a dimension is lost.

As the hawk with wings clipped, sooner would die;
Not meant to be earthbound, living to fly.

—RICHARD J. HARKNESS, *On Jets*
(by permission of author)

The Professional Pilot

. . . INTERPERSONAL RELATIONSHIPS, CREW COORDINATION

THE LIFE of a professional pilot can be exceedingly interesting and re-
warding. Unlike the monotonous routine of our desk-bound brethren, the professional pilot may make an instrument approach to minimums at Wilmington
in the morning and land under clear skies at Cheyenne in the afternoon. As
pilot for a major corporation you may fly to London, Paris, and the Mideast in
the fall and cover the entire Pacific area in the spring. One insurance company
covers a quarter of the United States every three to four months. And at the
end of the year the crew can speak of friends they've made literally all over the
United States.

It's a chancy business though. Airline jobs traditionally fluctuate with the
economy. And so it is with corporate employment of any kind. One company
may hire you at a good salary to fly their corporate airplane. After six months
the chairman, under pressure from the board of directors or shareholders,
decides it's too expensive and sells. You are suddenly unemployed. Also, in a
small flight department there may be no chance to progress. To move up to jets
from turboprops or light twins you may have to shop for employment in
another area of the country.

When getting started as a professional pilot you'll need commercial, instrument, and multiengine ratings and at least 1000 hr flying experience. In addition, the instrument flight instructor rating (CFII) is an indication of sound
knowledge of the ATC system. Many professional pilots come up the hard
way, starting as mechanics; this gives them an excellent insight into what
makes an airplane tick. Then they obtain commercial and multiengine tickets
and ultimately flight instructor ratings.

As flight instructors, new pilots have an excellent opportunity to reenforce
their own basic knowledge of flying by teaching others. Meanwhile they build
time toward additional licenses and then the ultimate, an Airline Transport
Pilot rating.

If you are a military pilot finishing active duty, you'll do well to go immediately after that ATP, getting the flight check either in a light twin or cor-

porate jet. Ex-military pilots must become acclimated to civil flying. Light twins do not perform in an emergency like the more powerful airplanes they have been flying. And jets require a different method of computing takeoff and landing capabilities.

As a civilian pilot you will decide whether to go or await better weather. No supervisor of flying or command post duty officer will be on hand to make the decision for you. In addition, while on the road you'll make your own preflights, check tires, and supervise refueling.

The Job Search

Finding a flying job is no easy task for the new pilot. If you are low on total flying time, look for a position as copilot. Most aviation insurance companies require that a pilot of a jet or prop twin have all the basic licenses—commercial/instrument, multiengine—and at least 1000–1500 hr total flying time, preferably in sophisticated aircraft. An aircraft and power plant mechanic's license is very desirable. However, don't expect to be able to maintain *and* fly. You can do superficial maintenance but you cannot serve two masters effectively. The low time pilot should spot the captains and chief pilots in the area. Most of them understand the difficulty in getting started and usually will help. They may not be able to offer a job but they will often help the newcomer build some substantial airplane copilot time (after proper training of course—copilot time without first receiving formal schooling is of little practical value).

Potential corporate pilots have essentially three ways to go about finding a job: (1) by keeping in touch with friends in the industry who may hear of a job; (2) by going through pilot placement agencies; and (3) by visiting airports and introducing themselves—many pilots have been hired when they appeared at an opportune moment. The larger companies however require interviews and psychological testing, which can take weeks; the job may also be more lasting and secure.

In common with most industrial positions, professional pilots have little economic security. This is true in the airlines, too, until a pilot reaches 12–15 years seniority. Consequently, it is prudent to keep yourself well trained and up-to-date. Since many corporate flight departments come and go with fluctuations in the economy, the pilot can expect a loss of income, flying proficiency, and any accumulated retirement benefits without warning. The professional pilot should therefore maintain some outside interest and skill to hedge against this situation and against loss of license because of physical problems.

Flight Department Management

A certain protocol should be understood by all members of flight departments. The chief pilot owes his supervisor a certain respect and loyalty, demonstrated by keeping the boss informed concerning basic management indicators regarding flight department activities.

The chief pilot or the office representative should know the location of each company-owned airplane and each flight crewmember at all times. A monthly (or weekly) report should show hours flown in *block time* and *air time.* Block time reflects pilot workload (ever hold for 45 min at the end of the runway?), while air time indicates aircraft usage and helps managers visualize the consumption of engine life, time to various inspections, and scheduled replacement items.

Nautical miles flown based on the flight planned route and the number of passenger miles flown are important statistics for evaluating the type of aircraft used and in proposing a newer, faster aircraft. The flight department must know the total flight hours, how many night and weather hours, and the number of instrument approaches each pilot has accomplished each month.

Crew duty time, daily flight hours, and amount of time available to executives during a working day are direct indicators of whether the company has the correct airplane for the job. For example, if you are spending 10 hr a day on the road (with 5–6 hr in flight) and your passengers are getting only 3 hr of business accomplished, too much time is spent in transportation and too little in working. A faster airplane is indicated.

Another consideration is maintenance reliability. If the airplane is costing an inordinate amount in maintenance, in both money and down time, a different airplane may be needed. Other possibilities are that the company is being overcharged for maintenance or the mechanics are inadequately trained on the particular type of aircraft involved. Whatever the situation, the aviation manager must be aware of these things.

The chief pilot should not air grievances with his supervisor to members of the flight department. It adversely affects morale and demonstrates a lack of leadership on the part of the chief pilot, who should be the shock absorber between management and department employees. Situations occur in which the VP operations, the company president, or the chairman of the board may be eccentric and have idiosyncracies that have a debilitating effect on the entire organization. However, the chief pilot who berates or gossips about the boss or other members of higher management runs the risk of being repeated in the executive offices by an overly ambitious captain or copilot who is jockeying for the position.

Conversely, the chief pilot should not carry tales to management concerning subordinates unless backing or approval is needed to institute recommended corrective action. Knowledge of various pilot weaknesses by nonpilot executives may result in a loss of confidence and jeopardize the existence of the entire department.

When someone in higher management causes continuous emotional turmoil in the flight department it is best to quietly and quickly find another job. A member of the flight department who creates personality problems should be promptly dismissed. To procrastinate is weak leadership. Remember, the lives of your corporate passengers are at stake, and emotional instability between pilots in the cockpit causes accidents. And too, you are not in the psychological counseling business.

The first responsibility of the pilots themselves is to the chief pilot. Jumping the chain of command is career roulette as well as transparent to mature management. Taking assigned projects to the VP operations for approval without clearance from the chief pilot indicates immaturity and a lack of understanding of the corporate chain of command.

A subordinate crewmember carrying tales of a captain's incompetence over the boss's head is another of the personality problems frequently encountered by the chief pilot. The copilot is in fact obligated to report evidence of a captain's incompetence to the chief pilot, who as department manager is the responsible official in the command chain. If flight department pilots collectively feel that a captain, a copilot, or the chief pilot is incompetent, a showdown with the operations manager or appropriate executive, accompanied by a number of documented incidents, is the final alternative. An incompetent individual should not be allowed to go unchallenged, since lives are at stake. But remember you are playing with possible legal action, so your facts must be carefully organized and documented.

The corporate flight department must be a pleasant, wholesome place in which to work. If working conditions are unpleasant and, because of an insensitive management, crew duty times are excessive, safety is compromised and the work effort becomes an active cancer. It is easy to make a serious mistake when you are emotionally upset or fatigued.

The deleterious effect of tobacco smoke on the pressurization system and instruments is good reason for the crew to refrain from smoking in the cockpit. Under no circumstances should cigars or pipes be allowed. The prohibition should be written in the company operations manual so that both crew and passengers are forewarned. Almost nothing is worse than opening the airplane on a hot summer day only to let your distinguished passengers discover that your multimillion dollar miniairliner smells like a bar on New Year's morning.

Chief Pilot Duties

The chief pilot should:

1. publish a management-approved Standard Operating Procedures manual with periodic revisions (also management-approved)
2. direct and supervise scheduling of all company flights
3. procure and schedule initial and recurrent training of flight department personnel
4. provide company management with periodic reports and statistics that reflect the cost of operation
5. prepare the department budget and review it quarterly
6. approve all flight department expense reports prior to processing for payment
7. maintain a monthly, quarterly, and yearly airplane and pilot schedule for orderly accomplishment of maintenance, crew training, and career development courses. This ensures compliance with FAA regulations and company policies and promotes individual development. The forthcoming month's duty

and pilot availability schedule should be posted at least two weeks early. The refined weekly schedule should be ready by at least the preceding Wednesday. For unscheduled trips a standby crew should be delegated daily.

8. ensure the protection and security of company aircraft.

9. maintain a pleasant operational environment (office, lounge, flight planning area, etc.)

10. ensure that flight personnel accomplish their job safely, courteously, and competently; and at the same time see that the crew is not abused or browbeaten by a particular passenger into excessive flying in one day or flying in conditions of severe weather. (This can occur when the executive is a former pilot.) Crew duty hours, weather, and minimum airfield conditions should be spelled out in the Operations Manual.

Crewmember Duties

Every flight involving multiple crewmembers must have a designated captain and designated copilot. The terms *captain* and *copilot* indicate areas of responsibility and work definition, not cockpit seating arrangement. An airplane can have only one captain.

Cockpit duties are designed around the pilot who is actually flying the aircraft and cockpit crewmembers must adhere to the specific duties assigned to their crew positions for that flight. The copilot has certain specific duties assigned and the captain has a specific area of responsibility. However, when the cockpit seating arrangement is such that the assigned copilot occupies the left seat and the captain the right seat, they each must perform the specific functions outlined for the seat occupied. In marginal weather conditions, or when operating from short runways or under maximum performance conditions, the captain should sit in the left seat and function accordingly. Together the captain and the copilot must have the training and ability to conduct a safe, smooth flight and to react in a professional manner when an emergency develops. Remember that the copilot is second-in-command.

The captain, as pilot-in-command, must never convey the impression that a supporting crewmember is managing cockpit activities or that the cockpit lacks leadership. The following concepts of leadership are paramount in the effective control of a crew of two or three. The captain must

1. completely understand the cause and effect of each step in a checklist

2. insist on the use of a challenge-and-response checklist procedure in a positive and professional manner

3. be positive in approaching problems, not vacillating from one random idea to another

4. preface each checklist with the correct title when calling for it, such as Before Takeoff Checklist or Before Landing Checklist. Nonstandard terminology has caused accidents

5. insist on intercrew cross-checking before accomplishing a normal or

emergency procedure that could shut down a vital system such as the electrical master, fuel selector, power lever, or fire "T" handle

6. verbally identify power levers, start buttons, and fire switches by their appropriate engine positon or number *before* activation during a critical emergency procedure; for example, announce "retarding the left throttle" or "shutting down the right engine" before you actually make the move

7. use an authoritative and controlled voice inflection during accomplishment of an emergency procedure

8. know and abide by the performance limitations and normal and emergency procedures as provided in the FAA approved Airplane Flight Manual. The captain is charged with this by law.

Ground Duties

The captain is responsible for:

1. the operation and security of the aircraft, equipment, and required records and documents

2. supervising and ensuring proper completion of the functions assigned to the copilot

3. ensuring that the departure and arrival schedule is known by maintenance and the FBO (fixed base operator), the cockpit crew, and the passengers

4. ensuring that each passenger to be carried is known and his or her name recorded by a responsible company official. On the road, call in passenger names to some designated company office or the flight department secretary

5. completing a navigation flight log, flight plan, and weight and balance form and checking weather, airfield conditions, and NOTAMs

6. ordering trip fuel and appropriate catering supplies (this is usually delegated after the appropriate decisions have been made)

7. ensuring payment for fuel, fees, and other services

8. accomplishing the passenger briefing as required by the appropriate regulation (FAR 91, 135, or 121)

9. ensuring that appropriate up-to-date navigation publications are on board and in the cockpit

10. reviewing log entries for accuracy and completeness at the end of the trip; ensuring that each aircraft discrepancy is recorded

The copilot is responsible for:

1. placing appropriate supplies and catering aboard the aircraft

2. assuring orderliness and cleanliness of the aircraft interior

3. determining the status and location of licenses, manuals, and navigation charts

4. supervising refueling for proper grade, balance, and quantity

5. checking passenger ground transportation arrangements at the destination airport

6. loading and unloading baggage
7. logbook entries
8. having the aircraft cleaned after the trip
9. covering engines and securing the aircraft during an overnight or extended parking
10. other duties as assigned by the captain

Flight Duties

Nothing can alter the responsibilities of the pilot-in-command. However certain specific actions and duties are inherent to the seat position occupied. The following activities are accomplished according to the cockpit seat occupied, i.e., left or right seat.

The pilot in the left seat is responsible for:

1. greeting the passengers
2. closing the entrance door
3. initiating use of the checklist and replying with the proper responses
4. directly controlling the aircraft during all phases of flight. During takeoff the hands of the pilot in the left seat must be on the throttles until reaching V_{mc} (minimum control speed) in a light twin or V_1 (decision speed) in a transport category aircraft (i.e., aircraft certified under FAR 25). Without a copilot the left-seat pilot will rotate with one hand on the wheel and the other on the throttles. With a copilot both hands should be used to rotate at V_R, while the right-seat pilot equalizes, monitors, and holds the engine power settings. During takeoff the left-seat pilot concentrates on aircraft control, such as heading, speeds, and rate of climb.
5. directly actuating any switches, knobs, or levers located on the left side of the center mounted throttle quadrant, although actuation (up or down) of the gear handle on the left side may be delegated to the right-seat pilot under certain conditions such as low visibility or a black night departure
6. maintaining engine synchronization for passenger comfort
7. controlling cabin and cockpit temperature levels
8. verbally verifying all elements of the clearance with the right-seat pilot before takeoff and during changing conditions in flight

The right-seat pilot is responsible for:

1. presetting cockpit avionics to the extent possible prior to start, and making subsequent frequency and transponder changes as requested
2. obtaining and verbally verifying ATIS (Automatic Terminal Information Service) information prior to start or taxi and prior to landing
3. reading the checklist and receiving the correct responses from the left-seat pilot before proceeding
4. recording start, takeoff, landing, and shutdown times; also recording the Hobbs meter reading (important at tax time)

5. logging the names and company affiliation of each passenger (also an important tax requirement)
6. recording each malfunction in the aircraft maintenance record
7. opening the entrance door and assisting the passengers in deplaning
8. assisting in unloading baggage and carrying it to the terminal or autos

The copilot, a fellow professional, is by law the second-in-command, with training thorough enough to be able to fly and land the aircraft on every other leg. The captain who insists on doing 100% of the flying is a very insecure individual; and the copilot quickly becomes unqualified to handle the aircraft. Copilot training requirements are spelled out generally in FAR 61.55. However, it is false economy to skimp on copilot training because one of the copilot's primary functions is to help prevent the captain from making a serious mistake; and should the captain become incapacitated for any reason the copilot must be fully capable of handling the aircraft. Where applicable, a type rating for the second-in-command is good life insurance.

PART TWO

The Takeoff Phase

The Go, No-Go Decision

. . . TAKEOFF PLANNING FOR LIGHT TWINS

T A K E O F F   P L A N N I N G   in light twins poses a special dilemma for the safety-conscious pilot. Unlike their transport category counterparts, there is no regulatory guidance to define what a safe takeoff distance for light twins should be. As they say in poker, "It's guts or better to open."

Normal two-engine takeoff distance is unfortunately the criterion used by many pilots, a habit acquired while flying single-engine aircraft. Because modern twins are spunky performers with both engines running, many believe erroneously that a 2000–2500 ft airstrip is adequate. But safety-conscious pilots, who value the lives in their trust, plan for that unforeseen contingency. Like the airline or corporate flight crews, pilots must calculate a minimum runway length for each takeoff based on the worst situation, in which an engine fails at lift-off.

Normal Takeoff

In a light twin the variables in takeoff performance can be surprising. It is possible to find your takeoff distance tripled because of density altitude and a tail wind component.

To illustrate, let's use the Cessna 310R, since it is typical of the high performance nonturbocharged twins. We'll be departing New Orleans Lakefront, elevation 9 ft (Fig. 2-1). The wind is calm and the temperature is 86°F (30°C). The Normal Takeoff Distance chart in the Pilot's Handbook (Fig. 2-2) shows that the takeoff ground roll is 1910 ft. To clear a 50 ft obstruction, such as trees or power lines off the end, will require 2320 ft of runway. Always include the 50 ft obstacle figure in calculating your runway requirement; even without obstructions, this gives you some safety margin for errors in weight calculations, changes in wind velocity, changes in runway temperature, an unreported runway slope factor, or variations in takeoff technique. When the 50 ft obstruction is used, this figure is referred to as takeoff *distance*.

In due course we reach Cheyenne where we intend to refuel. At CYS the elevation is 6156 ft. And once again the temperature is in the 86°F (30°C) range. A look at the Normal Takeoff Distance chart now will surprise you; ground roll at gross weight has increased to 3650 ft; takeoff distance will require 4550 ft. Both figures have doubled because of airport elevation and ambient temperature (in other words, density altitude). Keep in mind that use of airfield elevation is adequate for these computations because pressure altitude seldom varies more than ±400 ft from hot to cold extreme.

A tail wind component offers an even greater handicap. For example, on

FIG. 2-1. New Orleans Lakefront airfield diagram.

WEIGHT-POUNDS	TAKEOFF TO 50-FOOT OBSTACLE SPEED-KIAS	PRESSURE ALTITUDE-FEET	20°C (68°F)		30°C (86°F)		40°C (104°F)	
			GROUND ROLL - FEET	TOTAL DISTANCE TO CLEAR 50 FEET	GROUND ROLL - FEET	TOTAL DISTANCE TO CLEAR 50 FEET	GROUND ROLL - FEET	TOTAL DISTANCE TO CLEAR 50 FEET
5500	92	Sea Level	1780	2170	1910	2320	2050	2480
		1000	1970	2400	2110	2570	2330	2820
		2000	2240	2710	2400	2910	2570	3120
		3000	2470	3010	2650	3230	2850	3470
		4000	2740	3360	2950	3610	3170	3890
		5000	3040	3740	3270	4040	3520	4360
		6000	3380	4200	3650	4550	3930	4940
		7000	3780	4760	4080	5180	4410	5650
		8000	4240	5470	4590	5990	4970	6600
		9000	4790	6400	5200	7110	5640	7990
		10,000	5410	7640	5880	8720	6390	10,270
5100	88	Sea Level	1480	1800	1590	1930	1700	2060
		1000	1640	1990	1750	2130	1880	2270
		2000	1800	2190	1930	2340	2070	2510
		3000	1990	2420	2130	2590	2360	2850
		4000	2270	2750	2440	2950	2620	3170
		5000	2510	3050	2700	3280	2900	3530
		6000	2780	3400	2990	3660	3220	3950
		7000	3100	3810	3340	4120	3600	4450
		8000	3470	4310	3740	4670	4040	5080
		9000	3900	4930	4220	5370	4560	5880
		10,000	4380	5650	4750	6210	5140	6870
4700	85	Sea Level	1220	1490	1310	1590	1400	1690
		1000	1340	1630	1440	1740	1540	1860
		2000	1470	1790	1580	1910	1690	2040
		3000	1620	1970	1740	2110	1870	2260
		4000	1790	2180	1920	2330	2070	2500
		5000	1980	2400	2130	2580	2350	2840
		6000	2190	2670	2430	2940	2610	3150
		7000	2510	3050	2700	3280	2900	3530
		8000	2800	3410	3010	3680	3240	3970
		9000	3130	3850	3380	4170	3650	4510
		10,000	3500	4350	3780	4720	4090	5130
4300	81	Sea Level	990	1210	1060	1290	1130	1370
		1000	1080	1320	1160	1410	1240	1500
		2000	1190	1450	1270	1540	1360	1650
		3000	1300	1590	1400	1700	1500	1810
		4000	1440	1750	1540	1870	1650	2000
		5000	1580	1920	1700	2060	1820	2200
		6000	1750	2120	1880	2270	2010	2430
		7000	1930	2350	2080	2520	2300	2770
		8000	2150	2620	2390	2880	2560	3100
		9000	2480	3010	2670	3240	2870	3480
		10,000	2760	3360	2970	3620	3200	3910

FIG. 2-2. Normal Takeoff Distance chart (*Cessna*).

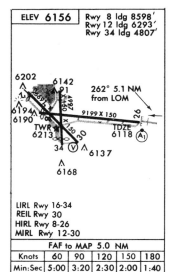

| ELEV 6156 | Rwy 8 ldg 8598' |
| Rwy 12 ldg 6293' |
| Rwy 34 ldg 4807' |

6202
6142
91
262° 5.1 NM
from LOM
26
6194
6190
9199 X 150
TWR
6213
TDZE
6118 (A)
34 (V) 6137
6168

LIRL Rwy 16-34
REIL Rwy 30
HIRL Rwy 8-26
MIRL Rwy 12-30

FAF to MAP 5.0 NM				
Knots	60	90	120	150	180
Min:Sec	5:00	3:20	2:30	2:00	1:40

FIG. 2-3. Cheyenne Municipal airfield diagram.

departing Cheyenne the tower gives us runway 34 (Fig. 2-3). Runway length is 4997 ft. No runway slope is listed in the Jepp's; however, this information is available from the airport manager, NOS (National Ocean Survey) charts, or FAA district office. (Ordinarily slope is not a major factor in takeoff and landing performance because most runways have a slope less than 2%.) Wind for this departure is reported as from the southeast at 10 K. We'll have a tail wind, but the runway is more than adequate. Right? Wrong! The aerodynamic rule is that a tail wind that equals 10% of the lift-off speed extends the takeoff distance 21%. In this case Cessna recommends an increase in takeoff distance of 5% for each 2 K of tail wind, which in our sample problem means a total increase of 25%. So, as we depart Cheyenne both engines must function flawlessly and the brakes must be held until full power is attained. With a 10 K tail wind, takeoff distance becomes 5506 ft, an increase of 956 ft.

The ground roll figure has increased to 4563 ft, which fortunately is less than the runway available. A misguided attempt to make a smooth rolling takeoff will add at least 500 ft to the runway requirement. You can visualize the result.

Accelerate-Stop

Now, what if an engine quits just as you rotate for takeoff? We'll abort, you say. But how much runway is involved? You can bet it is more than the Normal Takeoff Distance figure. We are now dealing with the most important consideration in light twin takeoff planning. Accelerate-stop distance is not required by FAR 91 for the takeoff runway, but it should be. If you lose an engine on takeoff without accelerate-stop distance available you are assured of an accident, and the survival aspects of a high-speed abort accident are not promising. Takeoff accidents account for 16% of our annual fatalities and serious injuries.

Again let's use our sample problem at Cheyenne. The Accelerate-Stop Distance chart (Fig. 2-4) shows that on a calm day, temperature 86°F (30°C),

WEIGHT - POUNDS	ENGINE FAILURE SPEED - KIAS	PRESSURE ALTITUDE - FEET	TOTAL DISTANCE - FEET						
			$-20^{\circ}C$ $-4^{\circ}F$	$-10^{\circ}C$ $+14^{\circ}F$	$0^{\circ}C$ $32^{\circ}F$	$+10^{\circ}C$ $+50^{\circ}F$	$+20^{\circ}C$ $+68^{\circ}F$	$+30^{\circ}C$ $+86^{\circ}F$	$+40^{\circ}C$ $+104^{\circ}F$
5500	92	Sea Level	3020	3190	3370	3550	3740	3930	4120
		1000	3220	3400	3590	3790	3990	4210	4490
		2000	3430	3630	3830	4050	4340	4570	4820
		3000	3660	3880	4100	4400	4650	4910	5180
		4000	3920	4160	4480	4730	5000	5290	5590
		5000	4200	4530	4810	5090	5390	5700	6030
		6000	4590	4880	5180	5490	5820	6170	6530
		7000	4950	5270	5600	5940	6310	6700	7110
		8000	5360	5710	6070	6460	6870	7310	7780
		9000	5830	6210	6630	7060	7530	8020	8560
		10,000	6330	6770	7230	7720	8250	8810	9420
5100	88	Sea Level	2540	2680	2830	2980	3140	3300	3470
		1000	2710	2860	3020	3180	3350	3530	3710
		2000	2880	3050	3220	3390	3580	3770	3970
		3000	3070	3250	3440	3630	3830	4040	4330
		4000	3290	3480	3680	3900	4190	4420	4660
		5000	3520	3730	3950	4250	4500	4750	5020
		6000	3770	4010	4320	4580	4850	5130	5430
		7000	4060	4390	4660	4950	5240	5560	5890
		8000	4470	4750	5050	5360	5690	6050	6420
		9000	4840	5160	5490	5840	6220	6610	7030
		10,000	5250	5600	5970	6370	6790	7230	7710
4700	85	Sea Level	2110	2230	2350	2470	2600	2740	2870
		1000	2250	2370	2500	2640	2770	2920	3070
		2000	2390	2520	2660	2810	2960	3120	3280
		3000	2540	2690	2840	3000	3160	3340	3510
		4000	2720	2880	3040	3210	3390	3580	3780
		5000	2900	3080	3260	3440	3640	3840	4130
		6000	3110	3300	3500	3700	3910	4210	4450
		7000	3340	3550	3760	3990	4300	4550	4820
		8000	3600	3830	4070	4390	4660	4940	5230
		9000	3900	4230	4490	4770	5070	5380	5710
		10,000	4300	4580	4870	5180	5510	5860	6240
4300	81	Sea Level	1730	1820	1920	2020	2120	2230	2340
		1000	1830	1940	2040	2150	2260	2380	2500
		2000	1950	2060	2170	2290	2410	2530	2660
		3000	2070	2190	2310	2440	2570	2710	2850
		4000	2210	2340	2470	2610	2750	2900	3060
		5000	2360	2500	2640	2790	2950	3110	3280
		6000	2520	2680	2830	2990	3160	3340	3530
		7000	2710	2870	3040	3220	3410	3600	3880
		8000	2910	3090	3280	3470	3680	3970	4200
		9000	3140	3340	3550	3760	4070	4310	4570
		10,000	3390	3610	3830	4150	4410	4680	4970

FIG. 2-4. Accelerate-Stop Distance chart (*Cessna*).

the accelerate-stop distance at 5500 lb gross weight is 6170 ft. With safety as a primary consideration runway 34 is eliminated. However runway 30 at CYC is 6691 ft long, and since it is almost aligned with our heading to Pocatello it is our second choice for departure.

But what about the 10 K tail wind? IFR (Instrument Flight Rules) traffic flow inbound from Denver necessitates a northerly departure unless of course you can handle an hour or more delay. Cessna has provided a wind compensation factor similar to that used for normal takeoff: "Decrease distance 3% for each 4 K head wind. Increase distance 5% for each 2 K tail wind." To find our new minimum runway length we must increase the no-wind accelerate-stop distance of 6170 ft by 25%, which is an additional 1543 ft. That no-sweat tail wind has extended the accelerate-stop distance to 7713 ft. Without this much runway and stopway (load bearing overrun) available, an abort at 92 K (engine failure or decision speed) will result in an accident. We are therefore relegated in our small, fast, Cessna 310R to runway 26, which is 9200 ft long. Hence the policy of some aviation insurance companies to require their insureds to have accelerate-stop distance, based on existing airfield conditions, as the "minimum runway length" for takeoff. And of course it must be paved. Keep in mind that in some twins, particularly in certain turboprops such as the Cessna 425 Conquest 1, the accelerate-go distance may be less than accelerate-stop. It depends on conditions. Remember that accelerate-stop distance is paramount. It is the *first priority* in flying passenger-carrying aircraft.

Accelerate-Go

First, light twins certified under FAR 23 (gross weight 12,500 lb or less) have *no* requirement for single engine takeoff capability. Some do have that capability; for those that have it the manufacturer provides a Single-Engine Takeoff chart (also called Accelerate-Go). It provides an idea of the distances involved.

Be very careful not to confuse the Single Engine Climb chart with the Single Engine Takeoff/Accelerate-Go chart. Single engine climb begins only after certain preconditions are accomplished, such as dead engine propeller feathered, cowl flaps closed, gear and flaps up, and best single engine climb speed (V_{yse}) achieved. Accelerate-go is accomplished at best single engine angle of climb speed (V_{xse}).

With no accelerate-go chart to guide you, remember that an engine failure before proper configuration and V_{yse} are attained means a forced landing. To paraphrase an FAA publication, at this point you are flying a single engine aircraft with the power plant divided into two parts. So when an engine quits, a forced landing is necessary.

Let's look at the accelerate-go figures for the Cessna 310R (Fig. 2-5). Again we'll assume a full cabin load and maximum gross weight takeoff. The distance obtained will determine which runway(s) are usable. This time we are departing New Orleans Lakefront airport. It is high noon and the outside temperature is 86°F (30°C). If an engine should fail at 92 K (our decision speed), we can accelerate-go using 4320 ft of runway. Our accelerate-stop distance is somewhat less, 3930 ft. These figures tell us that neither of Lakefront's two shorter runways can safely be used (Fig. 2-1). The normal takeoff distance is only 2320 ft, but the professional pilot is interested in safety. Therefore, even though the FARs do not require it, we must have a departure runway at least equal to our accelerate-stop. In this case, runway 18, which is 5889 ft long, allows a very comfortable choice to either stop or go.

Now let's visit Truckee-Tahoe, runway length 6400 ft and elevation 5900 ft. A quick check of the chart shows that, even on a 50°F (10°C) day, the 310R has no accelerate-go capability at its certified gross weight of 5500 lb. By off-loading fuel or passengers and reducing gross weight to 5100 lb (a 400-lb reduc-

WEIGHT - POUNDS	ENGINE FAILURE - SPEED - KIAS	PRESSURE ALTITUDE - FEET	TOTAL DISTANCE TO CLEAR 50-FOOT OBSTACLE						
			$-20^{\circ}C$ $-4^{\circ}F$	$-10^{\circ}C$ $+14^{\circ}F$	$0^{\circ}C$ $32^{\circ}F$	$+10^{\circ}C$ $+50^{\circ}F$	$+20^{\circ}C$ $+68^{\circ}F$	$+30^{\circ}C$ $+86^{\circ}F$	$+40^{\circ}C$ $+104^{\circ}F$
5500	92	Sea Level	2600	2850	3120	3450	3840	4320	4950
		1000	3010	3330	3700	4160	4760	5560	6810
		2000	3530	3970	4520	5250	· 6370	8080	11,540
		3000	4310	4990	5950	7520	10,350	------	------
		4000	5650	7020	9550	15,790	------	------	------
		5000	8470	13,010	------	------	------	------	------
		6000	------	------	------	------	------	------	------
		7000	------	------	------	------	------	------	------
		8000	------	------	------	------	------	------	------
		9000	------	------	------	------	------	------	------
		10,000	------	------	------	------	------	------	------
5100	88	Sea Level	2030	2190	2360	2560	2780	3030	3320
		1000	2280	2470	2690	2940	3220	3540	3940
		2000	2580	2820	3090	3400	3770	4230	4810
		3000	2960	3270	3630	4060	4600	5330	6430
		4000	3490	3910	4430	5110	6130	7620	10,430
		5000	4200	4820	5680	7030	9280	14,630	------
		6000	5350	6500	8480	12,550	------	------	------
		7000	7800	11,240	------	------	------	------	------
		8000	------	------	------	------	------	------	------
		9000	------	------	------	------	------	------	------
		10,000	------	------	------	------	------	------	------
4700	85	Sea Level	1600	1720	1840	1980	2130	2290	2460
		1000	1780	1910	2060	2210	2390	2580	2800
		2000	1980	2130	2300	2490	2700	2930	3200
		3000	2210	2400	2600	2830	3090	3390	3740
		4000	2510	2730	2990	3280	3620	4030	4540
		5000	2860	3140	3460	3850	4320	4930	5820
		6000	3320	3690	4130	4700	5450	6610	8370
		7000	3960	4500	5200	6190	7820	10,780	------
		8000	4990	5920	7350	10,020	16,800	------	------
		9000	7040	9510	15,370	------	------	------	------
		10,000	13,110	------	------	------	------	------	------
4300	81	Sea Level	1270	1360	1450	1550	1650	1760	1890
		1000	1400	1500	1600	1710	1830	1960	2100
		2000	1540	1650	1760	1890	2030	2180	2340
		3000	1700	1820	1960	2110	2270	2440	2640
		4000	1890	2040	2190	2370	2560	2770	3020
		5000	2100	2270	2460	2670	2900	3170	3470
		6000	2360	2570	2790	3050	3340	3690	4100
		7000	2690	2940	3220	3550	3950	4430	5110
		8000	3110	3430	3810	4280	4860	5720	6850
		9000	3690	4150	4710	5460	6610	8330	11,760
		10,000	4490	5190	6160	7730	10,510	------	------

FIG. 2-5. Accelerate-Go Distance chart (*Cessna*).

tion in the fuel load) we can maintain an accelerate-go capability; however, the single engine takeoff distance would consume an astounding 12,500 ft of runway. By further decreasing the fuel load to 4700 lb, the accelerate-go distance becomes a more practical 4700 ft. Note that when the outside temperature exceeds 68°F (20°C), it is no longer possible to accelerate-go at that gross weight. So careful timing of your departure in summer is needed to ensure that you leave during the coolest part of the day; 0530–0700 A.M. is usually best. Otherwise you'll have "a single engine aircraft with the power plant divided into two parts."

Turbocharging helps considerably by delaying the weight penalty to a much higher elevation or temperature. The more powerful nonturbo engines in late model aircraft also enhance capabilities. Don't forget that the charted takeoff and landing data were obtained under ideal conditions by highly experienced factory test pilots—engine and brake wear and the surprise factor were missing.

One word about runway slope and tail winds. The uphill and downhill slope of most runways is a negligible consideration since it is seldom greater than 1–2%. The aerodynamic rule is that a 1% slope causes a 2–4% change in takeoff or landing ground roll, depending on the type of aircraft. (Aspen, Colorado, for example, has a 2% runway gradient.) With a 4% change for each degree of uphill slope, takeoff would be lengthened by only 8%, or 440 ft. Taking off downhill, the effect would shorten ground roll by 440 ft. But add an 8–10 K tail wind and the takeoff distance increases 21–25%.

In short, assuming the terrain off the end of the runway is relatively flat, it is infinitely safer to take off uphill into the wind than to depart downhill and downwind. This applies to all airplanes—airliners, corporate jets, light twins, or single engine trainers.

Remember that a safe departure in a light twin requires careful planning of cabin load and runway available. (Fig. 2-6). If your minimum runway figure is based on normal takeoff distance, you are betting your aircraft and the lives of everyone on board on the reliability of both engines—a bet that the accident records do not encourage. The pilot should know the takeoff figures for every takeoff.

The accelerate-stop charts provide the best means of determining the minimum runway length you can safely accept. And above all, remember that a tail wind lengthens normal takeoff *and* accelerate-stop distances significantly. Don't let that second engine take you to the scene of an accident.

WEIGHT AND BALANCE

ITEM	WT.	MOM.
1. EMPTY AIRCRAFT		
2. PILOT AND PAXs		
1. PASSENGER		
2. PASSENGER		
3. PASSENGER		
4. PASSENGER		
5. PASSENGER		
6. PASSENGER		
4. BAGS — BAGGAGE MAIN		
BAGGAGE NOSE		
5. TOTAL WEIGHT before FUEL		
6. FUEL WEIGHT		
8. OIL — MAINS – gals.		
AUX. – gals.		
OIL		
9. TOTAL WEIGHT		
10. ALLOWABLE Wt. & Bal.		

LIGHT TWIN TAKE-OFF DATA

AIRPORT_____

PRESSURE ALT._____

TEMPERATURE_____

WIND_____

RUNWAY LENGTH_____

WEIGHT BEFORE FUEL_____

TOTAL WEIGHT_____

ACCEL/STOP_____ ACCEL/GO_____

V_{XSE}_____

V_{YSE}_____

TWO ENGINE V_Y_____

T.O. MANIFOLD PRESSURE_____

FIG. 2-6. Takeoff planning data.

Transport Category Airplane Performance

... CALCULATING TAKEOFF DISTANCE

T O   F L Y   transport (T) category airplanes (those weighing more than 12,500 lb and including all turbojets) is a whole new ball game. Now we have regulatory requirements for takeoff and landing weights that are based on loss of the critical engine. The maximum certified brake release weight is the basic guideline; it includes structural and thrust limitations based on a standard 59°F (15°C) no-wind situation at a sea level airfield. Since standard day conditions are rare, the captain is required by law (FAR 91.37) to evaluate each of the other factors that unbalance the field. These include high summer temperatures, a head wind or tail wind, runway slope, pressure altitude (field elevation will suffice), the available runway, and terrain or obstructions off the departure end.

After all factors are evaluated via the FAA approved performance charts, the takeoff distance, which includes an abort at V_1, or lift-off and climb to 35 ft, is known officially as the *balance field length*. Among pilots it is more commonly referred to as *critical field length*. A change in any one of the parameters unbalances the field, and the appropriate performance chart must be consulted for an adjusted takeoff distance (see Fig. 3-1). The new departure requirements must then be weighed against the runway available and terrain or obstructions in the projected takeoff path. If the performance charts have no figures for existing airfield conditions—such as a tail wind greater than 10 K, slope greater than 2%, field elevation too high (e.g., La Paz, Bolivia, has an elevation of 13,355 ft, well above maximum certified elevation for corporate jets), or outside temperature too high—takeoff is illegal . . . and unsafe.

The Federal Aviation Regulations that bind pilots to the FAA approved performance data are second nature to airline or air taxi crews. Every six months they receive a thorough indoctrination in FAR 121 Subpart I (airline) and FAR 135 Subpart I (commuter/air taxi), Airplane Performance Operating

STATION_____

TEMPERATURE_____

PRESS ALT_____

2nd SEC GR. WT. LMTD_____

RWY LMTD_____ RWY AVAIL_____

GR. WT_____ /STAB TRIM_____

T.O. EPR_____ /CLIMB EPR_____

REVERSE THRUST EPR_____

SINGLE ENG EPR_____

No. Flaps   T. O. Flaps (75/80)

V_1_____ Kts. V_1_____ Kts.

V_R_____ Kts. V_R_____ Kts.

V_2_____ Kts. V_2_____ Kts.

V_{FS}_____ Kts. V_{FS}_____ Kts.

V_{ref} (emerg. return)_____ Kts.

FIG. 3-1. Sabreliner takeoff performance chart (*Rockwell International*).

limitations. Not so well known or understood by many corporate pilots is that FAR 91.37, Transport Category Civil Airplane Weight Limitations, binds them to the same basic performance restrictions as their air-carrier/commuter counterparts.

Because FAR 91, General Operating and Flight Rules, is basic to all flying, in this discussion of T category performance we will use FAR 91.37, Transport Category Civil Airplane Weight Limitations, to explain takeoff and landing performance (Fig. 3-2). Here is a portion of FAR 91.37 that binds the pilot to the

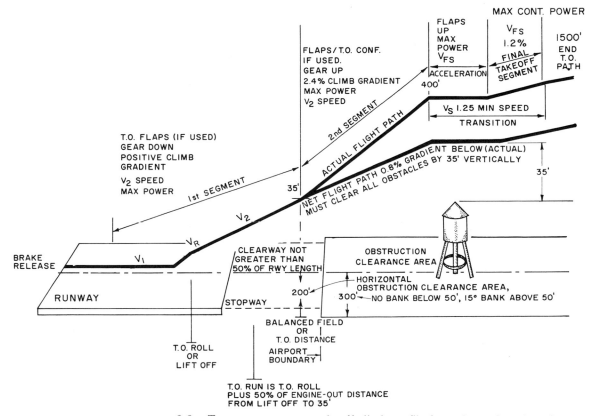

FIG. 3-2. Transport category takeoff climb profile for twin engine aircraft.

FAA approved takeoff charts: (c) No person may take off a turbine engine–powered transport category airplane unless

1. the accelerate-stop distance is no greater than the length of the runway plus the length of the stopway (if present)
2. the takeoff distance is no greater than the length of the runway plus the length of the clearway (if present)
3. the takeoff run is no greater than the length of the runway

A *stopway* is a load-bearing overrun that is strong enough to support the weight of aircraft certificated to use it should a high-speed abort become necessary. However, it is not stressed for regular use and cannot be used for takeoff and landing. A *clearway* is an obstacle-free area, 500 ft wide, that begins at the runway's end and has an upward slope not greater than 1.25%. This area must be under the control of the airport management.

A clearway is not useful in takeoff planning for most corporate aircraft because the performance charts give only one decision speed (V_1) for a given gross weight and flap configuration. This effectively limits the pilot to a runway that accommodates the accelerate-stop (takeoff) distance. For the larger airline jets, when a high ambient temperature, high field elevation, and heavy gross weight extend the takeoff distance beyond the runway's end, the charts provide for a lower V_1 to ensure the accelerate-stop distance required by the regulation (subparagraph 1). The remainder of the takeoff distance is accomplished over the clearway. The regulation, however, places specific limits on this.

When T category aircraft are certified under FAR 25, Airworthiness Standards: Transport Category Airplanes, takeoff distance is based on failure of the most critical engine at V_1. For a two engine airplane, one engine has failed. From V_1, using the balanced field concept, the aircraft can either abort the takeoff or continue to a height of 35 ft while covering the same horizontal distance. This is *takeoff distance;* some charts call it *Takeoff Runway Required.*

If takeoff is continued, the aircraft accelerates from V_1 to V_R (rotation speed). In some aircraft V_1 and V_R are listed as the same speed; this is permissible. However V_R can never be less than V_1. After rotation and lift-off the aircraft must be capable of climbing in ground-effect, with gear and takeoff flaps (if used) extended to 35 ft. Meanwhile the airspeed must be increased from V_R to V_2, sometimes called *single engine safety speed*, prior to reaching 35 ft.

Before going farther let's discuss two confusing terms, takeoff roll and takeoff run. *Takeoff ground roll* is the horizontal distance over the runway from brake release at full power until lift-off. The charts found in some of the early Sabreliner 40 manuals included both the normal two engine and single engine ground roll figures; later model Sabre 60s and 80s have only the normal two engine ground roll figures. Ground roll is not required and reflects a military requirement for the T-39 series. Most corporate aircraft flight manuals (T category) do not include ground roll charts.

Takeoff run is the minimum runway surface needed before a clearway can be considered. It is an academic phrase for pilots of most corporate turbojets.

The computation is made when an aircraft requires a clearway for departure. Takeoff run can be determined two ways; for brevity we address only the simple one. Ground roll with an engine loss at V_1, plus half the horizontal distance required to continue from lift-off to 35 ft is takeoff run. The computed takeoff run must not be greater than runway length. The remaining takeoff distance is completed over the clearway.

The entire takeoff certification procedure is designed to ensure that the traveling public is using an aircraft that is capable, after losing an engine at V_1, of accelerating and climbing at minimum specified gradients to 1500 ft, which is traffic pattern altitude. This is known as the *takeoff path*. From the charts provided, the airline dispatcher or the pilot can calculate the total horizontal distance in feet or nautical miles required to reach 1500 ft. By examining terrain features along the intended flight path the crew can be assured of an obstruction-free climb. If an obstruction is higher than the aircraft is capable of climbing in the distance available, then aircraft gross weight must be reduced until a safe climb gradient is possible. (A 2.4% or 1.2% climb gradient refers to a 2.4 ft or 1.2 ft increase in altitude for every 100 ft traveled horizontally over the ground.)

First Segment of Climb

While takeoff distance begins at brake release, the first segment of the single engine climb profile starts at lift-off (see Fig. 3-2). In this segment the twin jet aircraft must be capable of climbing with a positive gradient (0.3% gradient for three engine aircraft, 5% gradient for four engines), gear down, to an altitude of 35 ft. Simultaneously, airspeed must be increased from V_{lof} (lift-off velocity) to V_2 by the time a height of 35 ft is achieved. In actual practice the landing gear is retracted shortly after the aircraft is safely airborne; some flight manuals specify gear up within 3 s after lift-off.

With a marginal, runway brakes should be held until static EPR (engine pressure ratio) is set. Factory test pilots obtained the takeoff figures you see published in this way. Some aircraft may be so powerful that the brakes won't hold them at full power. If this is the case, a rapid throttle application is needed following brake release.

For passenger comfort most pilots make a rolling takeoff on a long runway. But remember that slow smooth throttle application can add 500–1000 ft to takeoff distance. In addition, if the pilot is too slow in applying maximum power, rated thrust may not be achieved at the target EPR because EPR increases as airspeed builds the inlet ram air pressure during takeoff roll. Consequently the pilot may stop power application at computed static EPR, and if the indicated airspeed has reached 80–90 K the engines will be producing something less than rated thrust.

With PT6A turboprop engines, power is reduced as airspeed builds to maintain a specific torque. In the pure jet, however, EPR is allowed to build as airspeed increases, up to a point.

TAKE-OFF RUNWAY REQUIREMENTS

ISA STANDARD DAY
CABIN PRESSURIZATION ON
ZERO SLOPE RUNWAY
NO FLAPS ANTI–ICE RAM AIR INLETS OFF
ANTI–SKID ON
DISTANCES – 100 FEET (V₁ – KIAS)

TAKE-OFF GROSS WEIGHT AT BRAKE RELEASE	TEMP. °F	TEMP. °C	SEA LEVEL (V₁)	1000(V₁)	2000(V₁)	3000(V₁)	4000(V₁)	5000(V₁)	6000(V₁)	HEAD-WIND KNOTS
20,000 $V_R = 129$	30	-1.1	50 (123)	51 (123)	52 (122)	55 (123)	60 (124)	66 (125)	71 (126)	0
	50	10	51 (123)	53 (123)	57 (124)	61 (125)	66 (126)	73 (127)	80 (129)	
	70	21	55 (124)	58 (125)	63 (126)	69 (127)	73 (129)	–	–	
	90	32	61 (126)	66 (127)	71 (128)	–	–	–	–	
$V_2 = 134$	30	-1.1	46 (124)	47 (123)	47 (122)	50 (123)	55 (124)	60 (125)	65 (126)	20
	50	10	47 (123)	48 (123)	52 (124)	56 (125)	60 (126)	66 (127)	73 (129)	
	70	21	50 (124)	53 (125)	58 (126)	63 (127)	66 (129)	–	–	
	90	32	56 (125)	61 (127)	65 (128)	–	–	–	–	
19,000 $V_R = 125$	30	-1.1	44 (118)	46 (118)	47 (118)	49 (118)	54 (119)	59 (120)	64 (121)	0
	50	10	46 (118)	48 (118)	51 (119)	55 (120)	59 (120)	66 (122)	72 (123)	
	70	21	49 (119)	52 (120)	57 (120)	59 (121)	66 (122)	74 (124)	–	
	90	32	55 (120)	59 (121)	65 (122)	70 (124)	75 (125)	–	–	
$V_2 = 131$	30	-1.1	40 (118)	42 (118)	43 (118)	44 (118)	49 (119)	53 (120)	58 (121)	20
	50	10	42 (118)	44 (118)	46 (119)	50 (120)	53 (120)	60 (122)	66 (123)	
	70	21	44 (119)	48 (120)	52 (120)	53 (121)	60 (122)	67 (124)	–	
	90	32	50 (120)	53 (121)	59 (122)	64 (124)	68 (125)	–	–	
18,000 $V_R = 120$	30	-1.1	41 (113)	42 (113)	43 (113)	46 (113)	49 (114)	54 (115)	58 (115)	0
	50	10	42 (113)	44 (114)	47 (114)	50 (114)	54 (115)	60 (116)	65 (117)	
	70	21	45 (113)	48 (114)	51 (115)	56 (116)	60 (117)	66 (118)	73 (119)	
	90	32	50 (115)	54 (116)	58 (117)	63 (118)	67 (119)	75 (120)	–	
$V_2 = 127$	30	-1.1	37 (113)	38 (113)	39 (113)	42 (113)	44 (114)	49 (115)	53 (115)	20
	50	10	38 (113)	40 (113)	43 (114)	46 (114)	49 (115)	55 (116)	59 (117)	
	70	21	41 (113)	44 (114)	47 (115)	51 (116)	55 (117)	60 (118)	67 (119)	
	90	32	46 (115)	49 (116)	53 (117)	57 (118)	61 (119)	68 (120)	–	
17,000 $V_R = 117$	30	-1.1	36 (108)	37 (108)	39 (108)	41 (109)	44 (109)	48 (110)	52 (110)	0
	50	10	37 (108)	39 (108)	42 (109)	45 (110)	48 (110)	53 (111)	58 (112)	
	70	21	40 (109)	43 (110)	46 (110)	50 (111)	53 (112)	59 (113)	64 (113)	
	90	32	45 (110)	48 (111)	52 (112)	56 (113)	60 (113)	67 (114)	72 (115)	
$V_2 = 124$	30	-1.1	33 (108)	34 (108)	35 (108)	37 (109)	40 (109)	44 (110)	48 (110)	20
	50	10	34 (108)	35 (109)	38 (109)	41 (110)	44 (110)	48 (111)	53 (112)	
	70	21	36 (109)	39 (110)	42 (110)	46 (111)	48 (112)	53 (113)	58 (113)	
	90	32	41 (110)	44 (111)	48 (112)	51 (113)	55 (113)	61 (114)	66 (115)	
16,000 $V_R = 112$	30	-1.1	33 (104)	34 (104)	35 (104)	37 (104)	39 (104)	43 (105)	46 (105)	0
	50	10	34 (104)	35 (104)	37 (104)	40 (105)	43 (105)	48 (106)	52 (106)	
	70	21	36 (104)	38 (105)	41 (105)	44 (106)	48 (107)	53 (107)	57 (108)	
	90	32	40 (105)	43 (106)	46 (107)	50 (107)	54 (108)	59 (109)	64 (109)	
$V_2 = 120$	30	-1.1	30 (104)	31 (104)	32 (104)	34 (104)	35 (104)	39 (105)	42 (105)	20
	50	10	31 (104)	32 (104)	34 (104)	36 (105)	39 (105)	44 (106)	48 (106)	
	70	21	33 (104)	35 (105)	37 (105)	40 (106)	44 (107)	48 (107)	52 (108)	
	90	32	36 (105)	33 (106)	42 (107)	46 (107)	49 (108)	53 (109)	58 (109)	

306–CL6–3B

FIG. 3-3. Takeoff Runway Requirements chart (*Rockwell International*).

Figure 3-3 is a Sabreliner 60 checklist chart that provides takeoff distance information. Remember that this information includes ground roll, an engine loss, and an abort or climb to 35 ft (first segment of climb). For elevations greater than 6000 ft, with a tail wind or runway slope, the flight manual charts must be used (Figs. 3-4, 3-5).

Second Segment

The second segment of climb begins at 35 ft altitude when the gear is fully retracted. Takeoff flaps, if used, *must remain extended.* Maximum power is maintained on the remaining engine(s). At V₂ the aircraft must climb to 400 ft

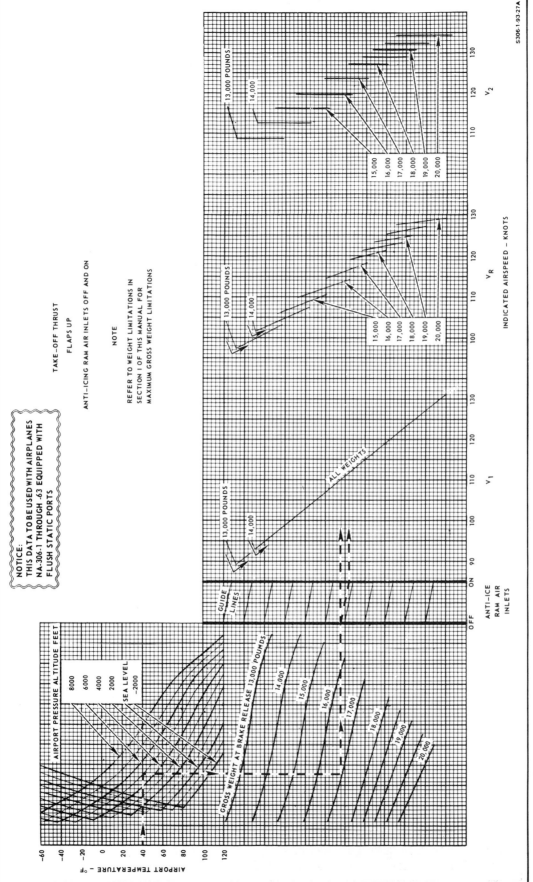

FIG. 3-4. V_1, V_R, V_2 speeds: cabin pressure on, antiskid on (*Rockwell International*).

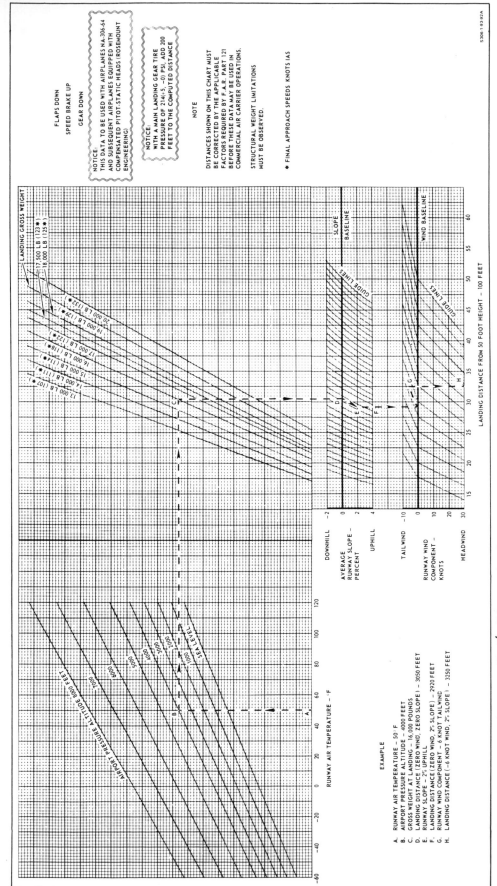

FIG. 3-5. Takeoff runway requirements (*Rockwell International*).

at a (gross) gradient of 2.4%. For the three engine Falcon 50 or Boeing 727 the climb gradient is 2.7%, for four engine jets it is 3.0%.

The net gradient shown in Fig. 3-2 includes a 10.8% safety factor that accounts for variations in pilot technique and allows the aircraft to cross over an obstruction at the end of the second segment or during the third (or acceleration) segment and clear it by at least 35 ft.

Most corporate jets have no problem with takeoff distance on today's metropolitan airports, intersection departures excepted. But as temperatures rise in spring and summer, a disregard of the second segment weight limit can jeopardize their ability to climb out of ground-effect following an engine loss. This is because most twin engine corporate jets are second segment limited; that is, they rapidly reach a point where ambient temperature and pressure altitude limit their capability to climb on one engine to 400 ft. For example, the Sabre 60 with cabin pressurization on begins to be second segment limited at pressure altitudes of 2500 ft or greater when the runway temperature exceeds 80°F (27°C). Some fan jets encounter this limit at sea level when temperatures exceed 85°F (29°C). (See Fig. 3-6.)

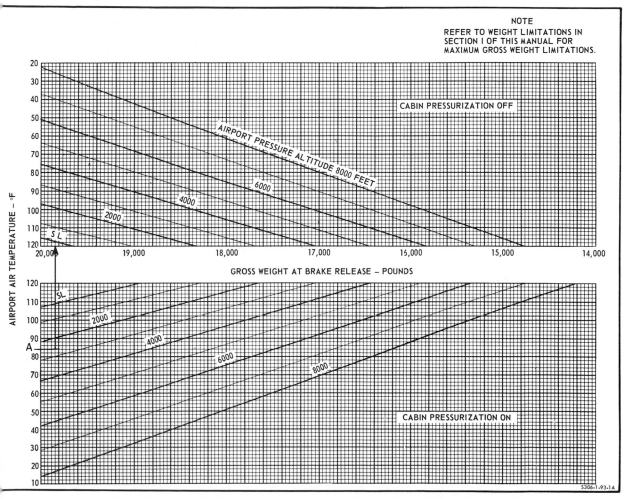

FIG. 3-6. Second segment limiting weight: antiice ram air inlets off (*Rockwell International*).

Final Segment

The final segment of the climb profile is accomplished in two stages. First, on reaching 400 ft, takeoff flaps are retracted and the climb gradient (rate of climb) is reduced to allow the aircraft to accelerate to its best L/D (lift-over-drag) speed—this speed is known as V_{fs} (velocity final segment). For the Sabre 60 it is roughly $V_2 + 50$ K, for the Falcon 20 it is $V_2 + 30$ K, and for the Citation it is $V_2 + 10$ K. Regardless of the aircraft type, the manufacturer cannot establish a V_{fs} slower than 1.25 V_s (25% above stall speed).

Maximum power is maintained on the operating engine(s) until the 5 min thrust limit is reached or V_{fs} is achieved. At this point power is reduced to maximum continuous thrust. Failure to accelerate to V_{fs} will result in the aircraft reaching the power curve somewhere between 400 ft and 1500 ft; drag will overcome thrust and the climb will stop. After reaching V_{fs} the climb is continued to 1500 ft, where the takeoff path ends. The distance traveled over the countryside to complete the climb profile is obtained by use of the Net Takeoff Flight Path chart (Fig. 3-7).

If the weather does not allow a landing at the departure airfield, the pilot must refer to the Enroute Net Climb chart. Preplanning the minimum enroute single engine altitude before takeoff, as required by FAR 121 and FAR 135, can be accomplished with this chart. It tells the pilot whether the gross weight of the aircraft will allow it to "clear all terrain and obstructions within 5 SM of the intended track by at least 2000 ft vertically" (see Fig. 3-8).

High Climb Gradient

An alternative to this relatively slow engine-out climb can be realized by tailoring fuel loads to the trip if you can rely on ATC not to replan your flight when you're number one for takeoff. On a cool day with a partial fuel or passenger load, many corporate jets have a high climb gradient situation. In this case an engine loss at V_1 proceeds as described previously except that the pilot retracts the gear and maintains V_2 speed until reaching 1500 ft (see Fig. 3-9). At that point, if takeoff flaps were used they are retracted. With maximum power still applied to the operating engine, the aircraft accelerates to V_{fs}. When V_{fs} is achieved or at the end of 5 min, engine power is reduced to maximum continuous and the climb profile is complete.

To find out whether you are in the high or low climb gradient area, refer to the Net Takeoff Flight Path chart of the Airplane Flight Manual.

Takeoff Weight Limitation

Because the Sabre 60 is typical of corporate jets (it has a great deal of power and weight-carrying capability), let's use it to illustrate a first and second segment weight limitation—most corporate jets are not limited in the final segment. For our problem use Hot Springs, Virginia, with an elevation near 4000

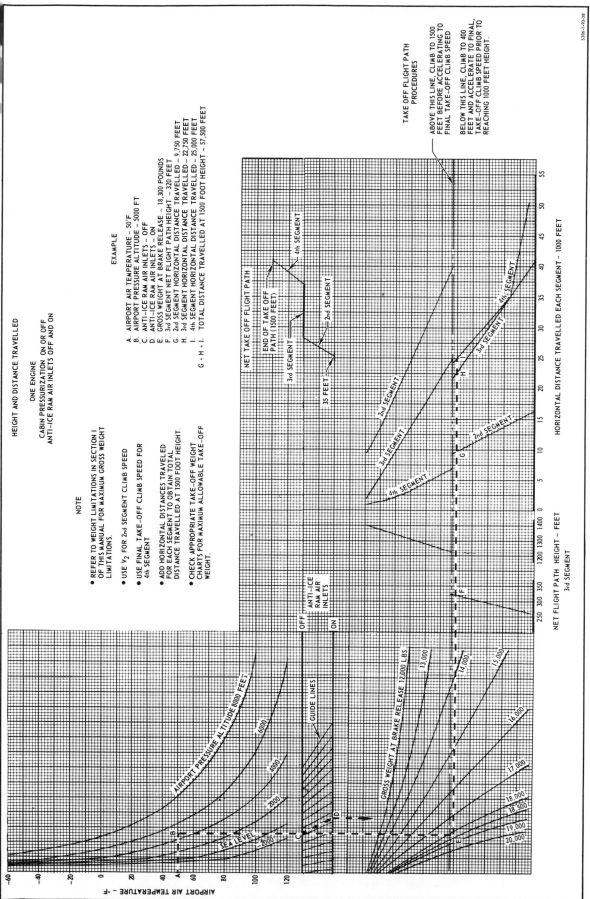

FIG. 3-7. Net takeoff flight path (*Rockwell International*).

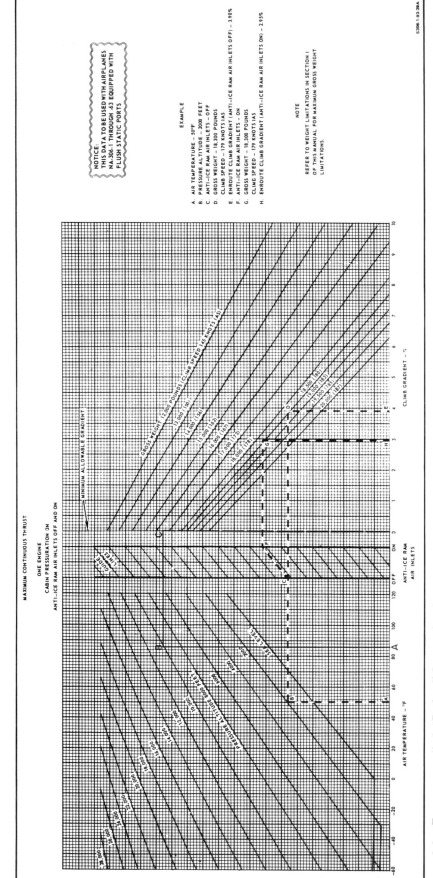

FIG. 3-8. Enroute net climb (*Rockwell International*).

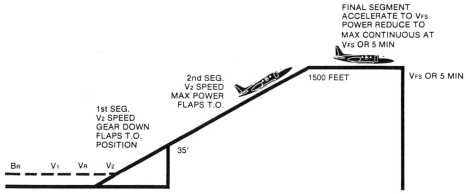

FINAL SEGMENT
ACCELERATE TO V$_{FS}$
POWER REDUCE TO
MAX CONTINUOUS AT
V$_{FS}$ OR 5 MIN

V$_{FS}$ OR 5 MIN

1500 FEET

2nd SEG.
V$_2$ SPEED
MAX POWER
FLAPS T.O.

1st SEG.
V$_2$ SPEED
GEAR DOWN
FLAPS T.O.
POSITION

35'

B$_R$ V$_1$ V$_R$ V$_2$

FIG. 3-9.   High climb gradient situation: cold and low pressure altitude.

ft. The ambient temperature is a warm 90°F (32°C). Because of airfield elevation and temperature we are suspicious of the second segment weight limit,
which is usually the limiting factor. Therefore, before ordering fuel we check
the chart for a weight limit (Fig. 3-6). Since we always depart with pressurization on we'll use the bottom half of the chart, and as expected the brake release
weight cannot exceed 18,460 lb. Since the Sabre 60 has a sea level takeoff
weight of 20,172 lb the elevation and temperature have unbalanced the field
and we must decrease the fuel load by 1712 lb or 256 gal. This is a reduction in
range or fuel on board of just under 1 hr.

We turn our attention to takeoff distance, because we are apprehensive
about the Hot Springs 5600 ft runway. The winds are (unfortunately) light to
variable so they will not help. When we obtain take-off runway requirements in
the checklist (Fig. 3-3), we discover that at 18,000 lb we'll need 6700 ft
(V$_1$ = 119 K) and at 17,000 lb we'll need 6000 ft (V$_1$ = 113 K). By continuing
down the chart we find that our gross weight must not exceed 16,000 lb to keep
our balanced field length (single engine takeoff distance) equal to or less than
the published runway length (5400 ft required at 16,000 lb). With a full cabin
load, giving us the maximum zero fuel weight of 13,800 lb, we are limited to
2200 lb of fuel or 328 gal. With takeoff and landing fuel requirements this is only 1 hr of fuel—a 3 hr range or fuel penalty. The relatively short runway at Hot
Springs has given us a first segment, or runway, limitation.

Let's switch the scene to El Paso, elevation also about 4000 ft. The
temperature at departure will again be 90°F (32°C) with the wind calm. We'll
be departing runway 9, which is 9000 ft long. As before, we first check the second segment weight limit and again it is 18,460 lb. To find the takeoff distance
we interpolate and arrive at a comfortable 7100 ft with a V$_1$ of 123 K—no problem on the first segment. We are not runway limited as at Hot Springs.

We are however IFR to Los Angeles. And because the weather is 2000 ft
ceiling and 3 mi visibility, an alternate is not required. To restrict the gross
weight to our calculated second segment brake release limit, we must limit the
fuel load to 4660 lb (696 gal). Since the flight requires 1 hr 45 min enroute we

have just enough to reach LAX (Los Angeles International) and, using long-range cruise, still have the required 45 min reserve. If the forecast weather goes below 2000 ft and 3 mi, an alternate airport will be required. We now have a range limitation and a refueling stop must be made. It is very tempting to add another 1000 lb of fuel and go nonstop, but imagine ingesting a bird during lift-off and being unable to fly out of ground-effect on the remaining engine.

Enroute Net Climb

After takeoff we declare an emergency and inform ATC of our engine loss. But no problem. Your last job was as an FAR 135 charter pilot and you became accustomed to planning a takeoff alternate in marginal weather. You've just departed El Paso on a 90°F (32.2°C) day but a thunderstorm with heavy blowing dust is fast approaching. Because you carefully tailored the gross weight at brake release you had no problem climbing to 1500 ft. Now you must fly airway V-19 to Frian intersection and land at your takeoff alternate, Las Cruces, New Mexico. However, the minimum enroute altitude is 10,000 ft; is the aircraft capable of climbing that high on one engine considering its weight and the warm ambient temperature?

Every FAR 121 or 135 flight crew must know the answer before takeoff; and so should every T category pilot. For this information we go to the Airplane Flight Manual and find the Enroute Net Climb chart (Fig. 3-8). (As mentioned earlier it is for enroute use above 1500 ft altitude to be certain you can miss enroute obstructions by the required 2000 ft.) To begin with we must know the ambient temperature at the altitude from which the climb begins. It is easily estimated by using the adiabatic lapse rate of 3°F (2°C)/1000 ft. The takeoff climb profile begins at an airport elevation of 4000 ft and continues to an altitude of 5500 ft, indicating a 4.5°F (3°C) temperature change (3°F × 1.5 = 4.5°F; 2°C × 1.5° = 3°C). Since the reported runway temperature is 90°F (32°C) we can expect 86°F (30°C) as we begin our single engine climb. (Note: some manufacturers use the temperature at the desired altitude.)

We enter the Enroute Net Climb chart at an estimated temperature of 86°F (30°C), (A); proceed to the required altitude of 10,000 ft, (B); and then move right to the minimum allowable gradient base line, which is a zero gradient, (C). (This gradient includes a 1.1% safety factor.) With a normal climb fuel burn-off our estimated gross weight at level-off is 18,000 lb. But we intersect the zero gradient base line well above the 18,000 lb weight line, indicating that we are Enroute Net Climb limited. To have a single engine climb capability to 10,000 ft our gross weight at level-off would be limited to 16,500 lb. It sounds complicated to new T category pilots, but it soon becomes a way of life if they learn the basics and conscientiously compute the data required by FAR 91.121 or 135.

One word of caution. Some pilots subscribe to a misguided theory that with an engine loss on takeoff the gear and flaps should be quickly retracted to improve the second segment climb. The gear of course should be retracted in short order, but retracting takeoff flaps could prove fatal. When you compute

V_2 speed using a takeoff flap setting you will see that it is about 10 K slower than V_2 with flaps up because V speeds are based on a percentage of stall speed. The flaps-up stall speed is greater than flaps-extended stall speed. When using a V_2 speed based on flaps extended, a sudden flap retraction places the aircraft approximately 10 K below the (flaps-up) V_2 speed. You are now behind the power curve, or drag exceeds thrust. At least one recent turboprop accident was due to premature flap retraction after an engine loss at lift-off.

Use of flaps for takeoff will shorten the runway (takeoff distance) required, but it results in a weight penalty in the second segment because of the greater form drag. So if you need to carry some extra weight, such as fuel or passengers, and have enough runway, make the entire takeoff without flaps. Keep in mind that a no-flap takeoff increases V_1, V_R, and V_2 speeds and increases takeoff distance. The captain must evaluate both factors and decide which penalty to accept. If you should be tempted to ignore the whole thing and rely on both engines to get you airborne with a full load, remember that 20% of accidents occur during the takeoff phase and most are fatal.

Slush Drag Deceleration

. . . CAN PREVENT TAKEOFF

S N O W, slush, or standing water on the departure runway can radically alter takeoff distance. It has the effect of unbalancing the computed balanced field length by adding an unprogrammed drag factor. Excessive slush or snow on the runway is a factor with which we've all gambled at one time or another. Usually it's impatience to get going that causes the pilot to ignore this recognized hazard. Sometimes it's caused by a lack of training emphasis. Some Airplane Flight Manuals establish a recommended maximum slush depth of from ½ in. to ¾ in. but many fail to address the subject, particularly those of light twins and turboprops.

FAA AC91-6A (5/24/78) provides excellent guidance for turbojet aircraft: "Takeoffs should not be attempted when standing water, slush, or wet snow greater than ½ inch in depth covers an appreciable part of the runway." Unfortunately not everyone follows that advice. In the winter of 1979–1980 at least two accidents were caused by this negligence. In one, a cabin class twin hit trees after takeoff, crashed into two homes, and killed both passengers. A third accident resulted in a sudden flameout of an engine with the pilot losing control. See if the situations sound familiar.

It was October 1979. The captain of a Westwind 1124 was departing Craig, Colorado. The crew had been stranded for about two weeks with an engine change due to ice ingestion damage that occurred on their last flight. After a successful test flight on Friday the crew called and received permission to remain for the weekend. They agreed to depart early enough on Monday to cover an 0900 trip from their home base, about 2 hr away. Unfortunately, sometime Sunday night a cold front moved through the area, leaving the aircraft coated with snow and ice. To make matters worse, it deposited 1½ in. to 2 in. of wet snow on the runway. Since the work force would not arrive until 0730 or 0800 the flight crew was in an embarrassing predicament.

The captain called home and explained the problem. He reportedly was told not to worry and to return to the hotel and wait for the runway to be plowed. However, the captain insisted that he could take the scheduled trip, albeit late, and would have to get the aircraft deiced first. Once again he was told to stay in place until the runway was cleared and another aircraft was scheduled to cover the 0900 trip. A short time later the Westwind rolled onto the snow-covered runway and attempted to take off. Unfortunately the slush drag was so great that the captain was unable to achieve V_R. Following a late abort the aircraft ran off the end of the runway, collapsing one main landing gear and incurring FOD (foreign object damage) to the engines and structural damage to the underside of the aircraft.

The second accident occurred on April 8, 1980. It involved a Cessna 340 at Crystal Airport, Minneapolis. While the final NTSB (National Transportation Safety Board) report is not yet available, preliminary information points toward a slush drag problem. It was early evening. Weather at the time was 600 ft overcast with ¾ mi visibility due to light snow and fog. Temperature was 33°F (1°C) and dew point 31° (−1°C). The wind was a good one, 350° at 20 K gusting to 30 K. An airport employee told investigators that he was working outside his home nearby and looked up when he heard the engine noise "to see who would be flying on a night like this." The tower operator reported that the aircraft appeared to rotate about halfway down the runway. It then settled back down and again became airborne at the end of the 3263 ft runway. Shortly after becoming airborne the aircraft struck trees, crashed into two homes, and exploded. The two passengers were killed. The surviving pilot stated that the runway was covered with 1–1½ in. of snow. The ambient temperature was 33°F (1°C) so the snow would have been quite wet. The pilot told investigators that he drifted left about midfield, held the aircraft down until reaching 105 K, and then rotated about 200 ft from the end of the runway. He hit the trees following a perceived power loss on the left engine. He had lowered the nose, he said, because the aircraft shuddered as if stalling.

Although the pilot was experienced, having more than 700 hr in the Cessna 340, his takeoff technique was completely wrong for the existing conditions. On a dry runway his ground roll using maximum gross weight of 5990 lb would have been 1510 ft with no wind and 1299 ft with a 20 K head wind. To clear a 50 ft obstruction—the trees he hit were reported to be 50 ft—his takeoff distance would have been 1724 ft. This distance is just over half the available runway. Unfortunately, by holding the aircraft on the runway to about the 3000 ft mark in an apparent misguided effort to achieve accelerate-go airspeed (105 K is 5 K greater than V_{yse} in the Cessna 340), he maximized the slush drag factors. He then failed to clear the obstructions.

In a third accident that occurred some three years ago, the captain of a Sabre 80 departed an Iranian airport with 4–5 in. of snow on the runway. Instead of following in the tracks of other aircraft that had departed previously the pilot began takeoff by plowing through fresh snow. Just after nose wheel disengagement at 80 K an engine suddenly flamed out. In the abort that followed the captain lost control and the aircraft was destroyed.

For starters, the term *slush* refers to water or wet snow. Because wet snow is less dense than water, the onset of dynamic hydroplaning and wheel spin-down occurs at a higher ground speed.

In the early days of jet transports, the airlines and FAA quickly discovered that an old chronic problem had become critical. With high V_R speeds, large dual and tandem wheels, and high thrust to weight ratio, the sleek new jets were very sensitive to water, slush, and snow on the runway. After several mishaps, NASA and FAA began studying the problem in an effort to eliminate this accident potential.

The first flight tests were accomplished using a Boeing 707 and later a Convair 880. Slush drag was found to increase up to about 70% of the calculated dynamic hydroplaning speed, at which point it begins to diminish. Once total hydroplaning occurred the wheels would spin down and slush drag diminished. The effects of slush on takeoff distance were found to be significant and are factors in the accidents described.

The retardation force of slush drag is proportional to (1) fluid depth, (2) fluid density, (3) and the square of the forward velocity (ground speed) until the onset of dynamic hydroplaning. For an idea of the forces involved, 0.5 in. slush increases takeoff distance 15% (Fig. 4-1). (For example, a 5000 ft takeoff distance at Hot Springs, Virginia, would become 5750 ft. But alas, the runway is only 5600 ft long.) If the slush depth is 1 in. takeoff distance is increased 50%. (A 5000 ft takeoff distance at Detroit City becomes 7500 ft, but the runway is only 5091 ft long.) With a slush depth of 1.25 in., takeoff distance is increased 100%. (At Spirit of St. Louis airport, a 5000 ft takeoff distance becomes 10,000 ft, but the runway is only 6000 ft long.)

Slush Depth	T.O. Dist. Increased
½ in.	15%
1 in.	50%
1¼ in.	100%
2 in.	precludes takeoff

FIG. 4-1. Effects of slush on takeoff distance.

The most significant finding was that with 2 in. slush the resultant drag overpowers engine thrust and the acceleration rate drops to zero. While the individual characteristics of each aircraft play a part, this result means that most jets would be unable to reach V_R with 2 in. slush. (No mention is made of prop airplanes in any reference source; however, they too obviously would have problems.) As a result of the NASA-FAA tests, the ½ in. slush limit was adopted for all turbojet aircraft—hence the recent reminder in AC91-6A, "Water, Slush and Snow on the Runway."

Of particular importance is the role played by flaps. Without use of takeoff flaps V_1 and V_R speeds become relatively high, increasing the slush-drag hazard (which also includes flap and gear door damage). Concurrently the higher V_R and takeoff speeds increase the impact of snow/slush in the wheel wells, which can mean gear frozen in the wheel well. Use of takeoff flaps lowers V_R speed but increases slush impingement drag on the flap surfaces. With double landing gear wheels, slush spray interference drag between

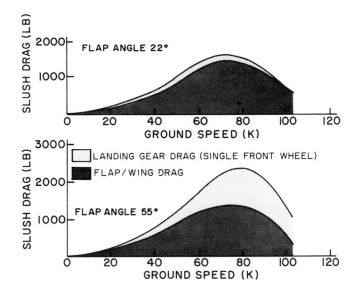

FIG. 4-2. Comparison of slush impingement drag at increased flap angles.

wheels is also a significant retarding factor. With takeoff flaps of 22° the relationship of landing gear drag and flap/wing slush impingement drag is easily visualized. Note in Fig. 4-2 that with landing flaps extended the flap/wing impingement drag is 70% greater than wheel displacement slush drag alone and flap damage is quite likely.

Tire Dynamics

A landing gear tire sitting static on the ramp is affected only by the vertical load of the aircraft weight. Tire pressure distribution in the footprint area is symmetrical, with the center of pressure located underneath the wheel axle centerline (Fig. 4-3, left). When the tire begins rolling at constant velocity (dry runway), (Fig. 4-3, center), it has, in addition, a drag load caused by the rolling

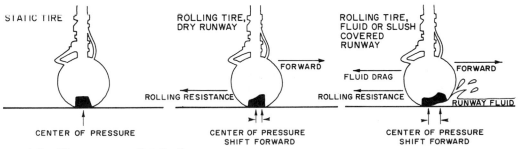

FIG. 4-3. Tire pressure distribution.

resistance of bearing friction, tire hysteresis (lag due to a change in force), and other effects. This drag load results in a spin-up moment about the tire that causes a shift of the vertical load to a position ahead of the axle centerline.

When slush is present, the drag produced by the tire displacing fluid from its path combines with rolling resistance and produces a larger spin-up moment that causes the tire center of pressure to move still farther ahead of the axle centerline. If the slush depth is great enough the drag force will increase sharply as ground speed increases (Fig. 4-3, right). Somewhere between 1–2 in. of wet snow will produce enough drag to overcome thrust, causing the aircraft at some velocity to stop accelerating. Even if V_R is attained, the drag from nose wheels and main gear may be great enough to prevent a successful rotation and lift-off. Conversely, with enough thrust to overpower slush drag and a long runway, at about 70–80% of the tire's hydroplaning speed the fluid begins to penetrate the footprint area, a hydrodynamic lift force is created, and the tire begins to spin down (Figs. 4-4, 4-5). As the tire begins hydroplaning, slush drag diminishes; however tire traction for braking and directional control will be lost. This also increases V_{mcg} (minimum control speed on the ground) due to lack of nose wheel cornering traction.

FIG. 4-4. Normal tire footprint with water dissipated by deep tread grooves.

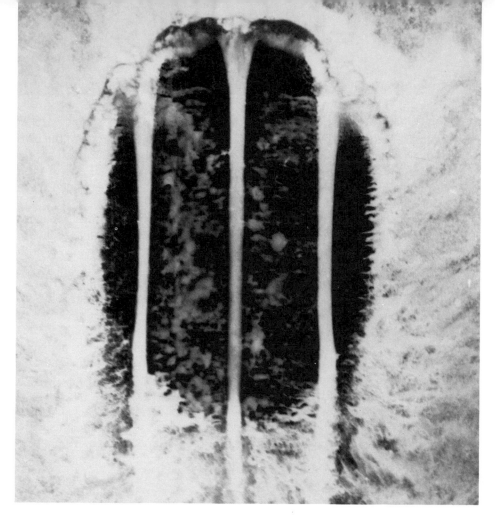

FIG. 4-5. Water film penetrates tire footprint and literally lifts it off runway surface as speed increases.

One more important consideration is the slush ingested by the engines. With runway temperatures colder than 41°F (5°C) and any accumulation of snow, slush, or water on the runway, the continuous ignition and engine inlet heat should be on. As the Sabre 80 accident shows, at slow speeds the slush spray pattern is weak, causing the nose wheel tire chines to deflect the spray directly into the airstream over the wing roots and into engine inlets. Tests on at least two types of corporate jets showed that the 70–90 K speed range was the most critical for engine slush ingestion. If continuous ignition is not used a flameout is likely. The use of continuous ignition usually results in a compressor stall although the engine continues to operate. The GE CF700 Cold Weather Manual recommends an abort if a compressor stall occurs before V_1. This is good advice, since you don't know whether you have ice FOD or simply slush causing the stall. Takeoff distance will also be compromised.

Engine Inlet Ice

When the snowplow has finished clearing the runway and the residual coating of snow melts at midday, puddles of slush may remain. In this situation the prudent pilot will depart with engine inlet heat on. Without heat the slush spray, especially if a crosswind is blowing it into one side of the aircraft, can hit the engine inlets and cause instant ice accretion. Then if inlet heat is added there will be the risk of ice FOD.

If the snow/slush depth is not reported the pilot-in-command must measure it. One jet engine manual gives 3 in. of moist snow as being equivalent to 0.5 in. slush; it depends on how cold and dry the snow is. Walter B. Horne (retired chief of the NASA Landing Load Track) uses a snowball test to guesstimate snow density. If it's wet enough to make a snowball, 2–3 in. will equal ½ in. slush. If it is too dry to make a snowball it may be light enough to reach 5 in. Wet or juicy snow should always be considered as slush.

On landing, three hazards await you with a snow/slush buildup: (1) hydroplaning; (2) slush drag deceleration from 6–8 in. moist snow can pop your nose wheel down suddenly and collapse a nose gear strut (it happened last year); and (3) flap, gear door, and speed brake damage can result from the high velocity impact of ice and snow. Remember that snow or slush packed into wheel wells can freeze brakes, gear microswitches, and landing-gear down locks. One Sabre pilot landed with only a nose gear because the two mains were frozen up, yet the cockpit indicators were all green. Some of the more popular turboprop models have had frozen brakes as well as the landing gear frozen in the wheel wells.

Remember the direction of FAR 91.3. "The pilot-in-command is directly responsible for and is the final authority as to the operation of that aircraft." Your decision to go rather than await better conditions can mean life or death to you and your passengers. Don't be "too late smart."

PART THREE

The Enroute Phase

High Mach and High Altitude Flight

... CAUSES AND EFFECTS; V_{MO}, M_{MO}, AND G LIMITATIONS

M A N Y professional pilots learn to fly the hard way, working their way up through the twins until finally becoming copilots or captains of corporate jets. But jet flying is a whole new ballgame, and alas, many of our training programs teach only aircraft systems. Yet systems failure has never been a major cause of corporate jet accidents.

To fly at high altitude safely the pilot must know a great deal about the Mach and airspeed operating envelope of the aircraft. Unfortunately these details are difficult to come by. From the manufacturer's viewpoint two factors are involved: product liability and competition. Who wants to advertise Mach tuck or shock induced flow separation? Unfortunately this lack of information and in-depth training in high altitude operations has resulted in fourteen corporate jet accidents over the past decade, including one in 1982, one in 1981, and three in 1980. Only one of these aircraft was able to land safely. Ironically *all* but the most recent were crew-only flights.

On October 1, 1981, a Learjet 24 was cruising at FL 450 on a flight from Casper, Wyoming, to McAllen, Texas. The ATC controller noted speed variations from .76M to .80M. In addition, aircraft altitude began to vary from $+200$ ft to -100 ft as if the pilot were using hand controls rather than the autopilot. Suddenly the controller noted an unannounced high-speed descent. The last altitude readout was made at 38,000 ft with a descent rate of 11,000 ft/min and increasing. Airspeed at this time was very close to Mach 1. The aircraft went into a steep dive and disintegrated on impact.

On board were three pilots. One was part owner of the aircraft and was thoroughly experienced in DC3s, DC4s, and the like; but he had only 22 hr of Learjet experience and no record of formal Learjet schooling, although he had recently obtained a type-rating from a designee in Dallas. The second pilot was also highly experienced with 17,500 hr in a variety of aircraft, including 5000 hr in the DC8. He too was type-rated with a total Learjet experience of 13 hr. The third pilot had been with the company only one month. His total time was around 1500 hr, all in light aircraft, and he was not Learjet qualified.

A similar accident occurred on April 11, 1980. A Lear 25, flying from Vernal, Utah, to Houston, was tracking at 41,200 ft on a 135° heading. Ground speed was recorded at 456 K. In a short period of time the aircraft changed heading and ground speed; then the transponder return was lost. The aircraft impacted in a nearly vertical attitude and exploded. The elevators, which separated at low altitude, were recovered some distance away.

Another mishap, which occurred on May 1, 1980, involved a Lear 35A cargo flight. It was 0100 EDT on a dark clear night. ATC tracked the aircraft's descent into Columbus, Ohio, at 458 K. It was on a heading of 090° with a descent rate of 1500 ft/min until about 21,500 ft. Meanwhile the copilot was in the cabin rearranging some of the cargo. Suddenly the aircraft's descent rate increased to 24,800 ft/min; and instead of leveling at an assigned 11,000 ft it descended to 8500 ft, pulled up sharply to 14,500 ft, and finally stabilized at 13,500 ft. Then the descent rate resumed at 1000 ft/min. During this episode the heading changed only 3°. The crew estimated their G load during recovery as 2–2.5. The copilot reported seeing approximately 450 K as the G forces peaked—V_{mo} for the Lear 35 at 8000 ft is 307 K.

The crew terminated the flight in a routine manner. During postflight inspection the left elevator was found to have separated and the right elevator had buckled. The crew reported an autopilot malfunction. The NTSB investigator theorized that the captain dozed off during descent with the autopilot off. He then overstressed the airframe during an abrupt pull-up from the high-speed dive. This conclusion was supported by the captain's demotion to copilot status by his company. The copilot quit.

On May 19 of that month a Learjet 25, with the captain in the right seat and an experienced though nontype-rated copilot in the left seat, disappeared into the Gulf of Mexico from 43,000 ft. ATC heard a crewmember transmit, "Put out the spoilers . . . can't get it up (pause) we're in a spin . . . oh jees . . . we're gonna . . ." Another Lear captain, flying 15 min behind at the same altitude and on the same airway, reported the worst clear air turbulence he had ever encountered. He had quickly reduced power and attempted to keep the autopilot and yaw damper engaged. Even though the speed increased from .77M to .80M, spoilers were not used. Cruise speed of the lost aircraft was estimated at .81–.82M. It and another Lear 25D operated by the parent company had illegal Mach airspeed warning cutout switches installed underneath the pilots' instrument panels.

In the early and mid 1970s two Learjets are thought to have crashed during runaway nose-down trim simulations. The first, in the Denver area, was a training flight with a highly qualified flight instructor. A cockpit voice recorder documented their combined futile efforts to recover from a high-speed dive. At Vickery, Ohio, the story was similar. A Learjet student was undergoing an FAA type-rating check. This flight, too, crashed in a diving attitude at high speed.

Some years back three Sabreliners crashed at high speeds in steep dives. All three occurred during IFR departures—two at night. From about 18,000 ft they seemed to have suddenly reversed course and impacted at very high speeds. One hit in the Pacific Ocean. The other two impacted terrain at very steep dive angles. Although runaway trim was considered, speculation favored vertigo following an autopilot disengagement or total electrical failure. The result was a near split S maneuver.

Mach Effect

An airplane's indicated airspeed limit is V_{mo}—*velocity, maximum operation.* When V_{mo} is exceeded aerodynamic flutter and G (gravity) limitations during dive become critical.

The aircraft's maxium certified mach number is M_{mo}—*Mach, maximum operation.* With an intentional or accidental excursion past M_{mo}, Mach induced flow separation of boundary layer air over ailerons and elevators results in a loss of control surface authority and buzz, coupled with a very dangerous phenomenon called Mach tuck. Mach tuck is common to most corporate jets, with certain specific exceptions.

A pressure disturbance in the atmosphere, whether caused by a gunshot, thunderclap, or moving airfoil, is transmitted by molecular collisions. A molecule so disturbed pushes against another, which pushes against a third, and so forth. The speed at which these collisions occur is the speed of sound. Mach 1 is the measurement used to identify this speed, which is 762 mi/hr or 661.7 K at sea level (15°C). The speed of sound is solely a function of air temperature. The colder the temperature, the slower the speed. Compressibility is a function of air density (altitude). Because of thrust and fuel (range) considerations, modern corporate and airline jet transports (the Concorde excepted) cruise at some percentage of Mach 1.

Wing sweep or shape determines the most economical cruise Mach number. A wing with 28–30° of sweep can cruise economically at .75M (75% of Mach 1) in the troposphere, designated as beginning at 36,089 ft by the ICAO (International Civil Aviation Organization) standard atmosphere chart. With 35° of sweep the same wing shape may be just as efficient at .84M.

At low Mach numbers aerodynamic friction drag constitutes the major portion of an airfoil's drag. As airspeed increases, airflow over the wing accelerates until at some point the local Mach number becomes sonic, that is, Mach 1 (see Fig. 5-1). This airspeed is the wing's critical Mach number, M_{crit}.

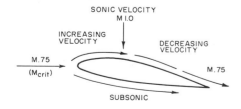

FIG. 5-1. Local Mach number becomes sonic at M_{crit}.

Airflow acceleration from subsonic to supersonic is smooth if the surface is smooth and the transition gradual.

As the airflow continues down and over the wing's contour it begins to decelerate. On the aft portion of the airfoil, where the airflow decelerates from supersonic to subsonic, a normal shock wave forms (see Fig. 5-2). As airspeed continues to increase, the shock wave becomes stronger and begins to act as a barrier to the local boundary layer air. It produces turbulence behind the shock wave, which in turn causes buffet or control surface buzz. In addition drag increases rapidly (see Fig. 5-3). This drag increase is not great at first; but at some point, usually 5–10% above M_{crit}, drag rises sharply. This point is variously called *drag divergence, force divergence,* or *drag rise Mach* (see Fig. 5-4).

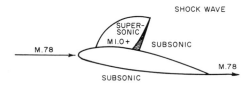

FIG. 5-2. Normal shock wave.

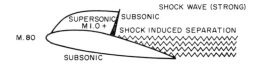

FIG. 5-3. Shock wave acts as barrier.

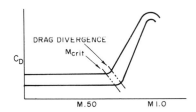

FIG. 5-4. Drag divergence.

In most corporate jets Recommended Cruise or Normal Cruise charts are based on a cruise Mach number very close to M_{crit} at or above the tropopause (FL 370). In the older sweptwing fleet it is .75M–.77M.

High-Speed Cruise or Maximum Thrust Cruise charts (assuming adequate thrust to weight ratio) are based on a Mach number just short of drag divergence. Interestingly, with 25–30° of wing sweep, this figure is usually .8M or .81M, and because of certain design features it is also M_{mo}. A higher Mach usually results in control surface buffet (buzz) and Mach tuck (pitchdown) in addition to drag divergence and increased fuel consumption. (The Falcon series, with irreversible hydraulic boosted flight controls, does not experience buzz or tuck.)

Mach Buffet or Buzz

Mach buffet or control surface buzz is a warning of danger to come. To make certain the crew is aware of this potential danger FAR 91.49 requires an operational Mach and airspeed warning system. The hazard involves a phenomenon known as *shock induced flow separation.* At around .82M the boundary layer air lacks sufficient energy to penetrate the shock wave and flow smoothly over the airfoil's trailing edge (see Fig. 5-5). Turbulence behind the shock causes control surface buzz in the early stages and loss of aileron and elevator effectiveness as the shock wave effectively dams the boundary layer air (see Fig. 5-6). The airstream's kinetic energy is then converted to a pressure and temperature increase behind the shock wave.

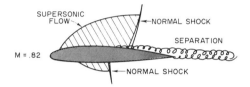

FIG. 5-5. Shock induced flow separation.

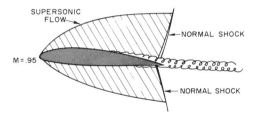

FIG. 5-6. Shock wave has effectively dammed boundary layer air.

Pilot ignorance of these facts has resulted in Learjets accumulating the worst high-speed accident rate in the fleet. The sleek fighterlike shape of the Lear has led some pilots to ignore certified airspeed and Mach limitations. The practice became so widespread that a so-called go-fast switch was being covertly installed, contrary to FAA regulations, to simplify disabling of the Mach and airspeed warning system, thus allowing flight at speeds greater than the certified limit.

In the Learjet series aileron activity (buzz) begins shortly after exceeding M_{mo}. Higher speeds increase the aileron and control wheel movement, producing *aileron snatch.* Abruptly pulling Gs to get the nose up only intensifies the problem. Instead, power must be reduced to idle and a steady back pressure applied to pull as much G force as possible (not more than 1.5 G) without losing roll control. One demonstration of this in the Flight Safety simulator will make a believer out of anyone. Aileron snatch (control wheel oscillating rapidly from side to side) can also occur in the Sabres 40, 60, and 80 during overspeed excursions when pulled into buffet. (The 60A and 80A, with the Raisbeck wing, exhibit only moderate aileron buzz even at overspeeds beyond Mach .90.)

Mach Tuck

Mach tuck is also a by-product of shock induced flow separation. Two basic factors are involved. The first is the shock induced flow separation that begins near the thick wing root; it causes a decrease in downwash over the tail, producing a nose-down tendency. The second and perhaps most important factor is the aft movement of the wing's center of pressure (aerodynamic center), which unbalances the subsonic equilibrium maintained with the aircraft's center of gravity. It too causes a strong diving tendency. Consequently several corporate jets have a trim or autopilot Mach compensator (stick puller) to protect the crew from an inadvertent excursion over M_{mo}.

The Raisbeck wing on the Sabres 60A, 80A, and 65 encounters *Mach pitch*. This supercritical swept wing has a drooped leading edge with a downward twist toward the tip that improves low-speed characteristics. The increased (tip) camber causes wing tips to "shock" first. As Mach number increases the tips download or produce negative lift; with the flexible tips twisting downward a trim tab effect is produced, causing a gentle nose-up tendency as M_{mo} is exceeded.

The Falcon 50 is different from both of these types. It has a neutral stability at high Mach numbers. It neither tucks nor pitches. Therefore French authorities wanted a positive stability, something to pull the nose up as M_{mo} was approached. Consequently a Mach trim system, which initiates nose-up trim at M.78–.82M, was installed. Thus if a turbulence upset induces a nose-down pitching moment, the aircraft will tend to return to its previous trim attitude rather than remain nose low with airspeed continuing to build.

Wing Design

Sweeping the wings is one method used to increase the critical Mach number and thus delay the adverse effects of high Mach flight. Degree of sweep is the angle of the quarter chord line with a line perpendicular to the aircraft's centerline. Whether they are swept forward or aft the effect is the same. However an aft sweep has presented fewer problems to date. For example, a straight wing airplane has an M_{crit} of .7. By sweeping the wings 30°, M_{crit} would be increased to .75 (see Fig. 5-7). A sweep of 28–30° is needed before any significant improvement is achieved.

Another method of increasing a wing's critical Mach is found on the straight wing Learjet. It has a modified high-speed laminar flow airfoil (see Fig. 5-8). This high-speed section wing has a small leading edge radius combined with a reduced thickness ratio. Instead of a curvature that produces maximum lift at around the 40% chord, it is tapered with its maximum thickness point moved aft. This arrangement distributes the pressures and boundary layer air more evenly along the chord, reducing local flow velocities at high Mach numbers.

To delay the onset of Mach buzz and thus realize a higher M_{mo}, Learjet uses both vortex generators and small triangular upper wing strips called *boundary layer energizers.* Both systems work well although energizers produce less drag (Fig. 5-9).

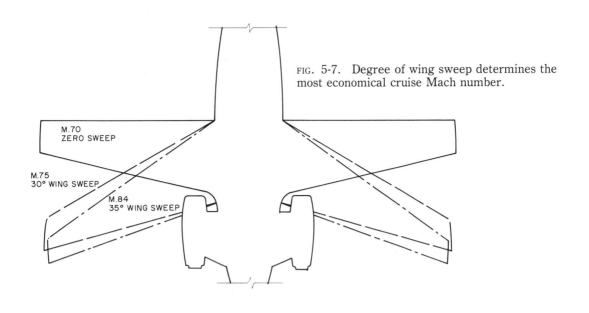

FIG. 5-7. Degree of wing sweep determines the most economical cruise Mach number.

M.70
ZERO SWEEP

M.75
30° WING SWEEP

M.84
35° WING SWEEP

FIG. 5-8. High-speed section (Laminar flow) wing.

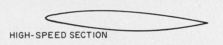

HIGH-SPEED SECTION

FIG. 5-9. Vortex generator vanes.

Vortex generators, small vanes about 1–2 in. high that rise above the boundary layer air, deflect higher energy air downward to accelerate the boundary layer aft of the still weak shock wave. This delays flow separation (aileron buzz) and thus permits a higher M_{mo}.

Supercritical Wing

Today's corporate jets utilize a supercritical (also called computer designed) wing (see Fig. 5-10). It is a relatively thick wing that provides low takeoff and landing speed plus space for additional fuel. By shaping it to modify pressure patterns, high cruise speeds are achieved without a significant drag rise. For example, the computer designed wing of the Falcon 10 allows it to cruise at .85M without encountering drag divergence.

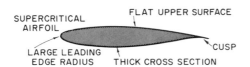

FIG. 5-10.   Supercritical wing

Coffin Corner

The trend toward certification of corporate jets to 51,000 ft has mixed benefits. The advantage is that now you can fly above the jet stream westbound and over all but a few thunderstorms. The disadvantage is that the low-speed and high-speed buffet boundaries begin to converge, which means that even a small change in speed (faster or slower) can become a serious problem. Since there have been no survivors in the high-speed corporate jet accidents, an airline incident will illustrate the problem. This incident involved the cirrus overhang of a thunderstorm; but keep in mind that even clear air turbulence, especially in the ultrahigh altitudes, can end your career.

A Boeing 720 had initiated a climb from FL 370 to FL 410 in an effort to top a cloud layer. They were in an 85 K jet stream with radar showing one "fuzzy" thunderstorm 30–40 mi away. Suddenly the aircraft pitched up to very near vertical, even though both pilots were holding full forward elevator. In a series of up-and-down drafts the pitch attitudes were steep enough to cause the horizon bar to disappear behind the top and bottom of the indicator. During this incident both the high-speed and low-speed buffet boundaries were encountered. At one point the aircraft was thought to have been fully stalled. Minimum recorded airspeed was 213 K and .69M; maximum speed was beyond 470 KIAS and .93M. (The recorder pegged at 460 KIAS.) The maximum altitude achieved was 39,000 ft. Dive recovery was completed at 12,000 ft. The recorder showed G loads of +3.2 G and −1.4 G.

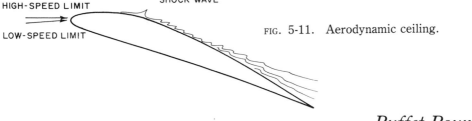

HIGH-SPEED LIMIT

LOW-SPEED LIMIT

SHOCK WAVE

FIG. 5-11. Aerodynamic ceiling.

Buffet Boundary

Every airfoil has an aerodynamic ceiling, which is primarily a function of shape and sweep. No amount of thrust can force an airplane above the aerodynamic ceiling of its wing because the high-speed and low-speed buffet boundaries have merged (see Fig. 5-11).

In the Falcon 50, which has irreversible hydraulic boosted flight controls, high-speed buffet is simply a staccato or washboard effect from the airstream. It begins shortly after M_{mo} of .86M is exceeded. In jets having conventional cable-pully flight controls, an overspeed results in control surface buzz (or snatch) combined with Mach tuck. (Mach tuck is not found in the Sabres 40, 60, and 80.) In some instances it may be accompanied by *control force reversal* due to increasing strength of the shock wave. In addition the aerodynamic forces on elevators and ailerons increase significantly.

Low-speed buffet is basically prestall buffet. Stall speed increases with altitude at a relatively modest rate until in the upper altitudes when it suddenly increases sharply (see Fig. 5-12) because of a decreasing Reynolds number

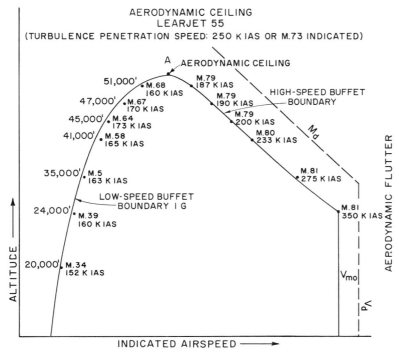

FIG. 5-12. Low-speed and high-speed buffet boundaries, indicated airspeeds obtained by interpolation. (Note: In turbulence low-speed buffet boundary begins roughly at 1.25–1.5 G above 40,000 ft. It varies with gross weight and wing design.)

(combined effects of velocity, distance from the leading edge, density, etc.) coupled with an increased angle of attack. This greater angle of attack causes leading edge airflow to accelerate prematurely and form a small shock wave.

At some point, the high-speed and low-speed buffet boundaries intersect, that is, occur at the same IAS (Fig. 5-12). In other words, the higher you fly the closer you are to the combined hazards of stall and compressibility. This is why clear air or thunderstorm turbulence is so dangerous at high altitudes in our Mach-limited corporate jets. (Engine flameout due to compressor stall is another common occurrence.)

A heavy gross weight causes a significant decrease in the buffet margin at a given speed and altitude. This is yet another reason not to carry too much fuel. You'll have the widest buffet-free speed range at light gross weights. High gross weights also affect G load capability, which means less tolerance to gusts before either an airframe overstress or low-speed buffet is encountered.

Turbulence Effect

Most of the time corporate jets have a comfortable margin from the 1 G buffet boundary. But above FL 390 almost every airplane encounters low-speed buffet at around +1.5 G. At FL 410 and above, about +1.25 G will initiate buffet in most aircraft. Since G load in a level turn is a function of bank angle, aircraft certified to FL 510 (for instance, the Lear 55) have autopilots equipped with a half bank function that limits bank angle to 15° above FL 450. If you try to follow the V bars with a normal 25° bank angle at say FL 470 while at a cruise Mach of .75, you'll immediately encounter low-speed buffet. This illustrates how close you are to the low-speed buffet boundary.

Suppose you are topping a line of thunderstorms that rise to about 42,000 ft. Your basic weather training cautions of severe turbulence (and possibly hail) at 1000 ft above a cell. Despite this you press along at FL 430 and M_{mo} of .79. About halfway across the squall line you encounter severe downdrafts that cause you to pull back hard on the yoke—1½ to 1¾ Gs—in an effort to hold altitude and avoid entering that ugly bumper. The aircraft is immediately deep into low-speed buffet that may even actuate the stick pusher. Inside the storm you encounter severe updrafts and, with the yoke going forward, the Mach warning horn and stick puller activate. Alas, if Mach warning has been disabled your first clue will be aileron snatch and Mach tuck. Now you are along for the ride—so long as it lasts. While severe clear air turbulence was involved in the Lear 25C crash into the Gulf of Mexico, this is almost the exact scenario given by the NTSB as to probable cause. Above FL 450 the problem becomes progressively more critical.

The area between high-speed and low-speed buffet is best measured by indicated airspeed. Figure 5-12 shows the buffet-free range (1 G) for a sample airplane at FL 350 to be 163 KIAS to 275 KIAS. At FL 450 the spread is only one-fourth of that, 173 KIAS to 200 KIAS. This information is important only if moderate to severe clear air turbulence or thunderstorms are encountered. The manufacturer has provided both an IAS and Mach number for best turbulence penetration. In the Lear 55, it is 250 KIAS or Mach .73, whichever is higher. This provides the widest margin possible between high-speed and low-speed buffet boundaries and other structural considerations (i.e., V_n diagram used by the manufacturer; see FAR 25.333).

Wave Pattern

Another unexpected situation that can lead to an overspeed excursion in high-speed cruise is the *standing wave* often found in perfectly smooth air. It is common in winter over mountainous areas, especially following passage of a cold front. A wave pattern can extend for more than 100 mi downwind from a mountain range and it is also prevalent above strong thunderstorms. In both cases it may be marked by cirrus clouds. On entering a standing wave, if the autopilot holds an assigned altitude in a downdraft the IAS will decrease, possibly to the point at which you enter low-speed buffet. Then IAS increases rapidly as the updraft is encountered. With the Mach warning system engaged you'll quickly get overspeed warning and stick puller activation. But if this warning system is disabled you may suddenly encounter control surface buzz (or aileron snatch) and Mach tuck. And once deep enough into Mach tuck you may have lost control forever.

Remember, the higher you fly the more critical the problem becomes. And you *can* get clear air, standing wave, or thunderstorm turbulence at FL 510.

Turbulence Penetration Speed

Most older corporate jets have a turbulence penetration speed of around .7M or 225 KIAS, whichever is faster. This speed is generally high enough to prevent a gust induced stall and yet slow enough to preclude overstress or structural failure. The captain must pay close attention to the turbulence penetration speed if moderate to severe turbulence is reported or forecast.

On the low-speed side, some T tailed jets have very dangerous characteristics at full stall. They include wing drop and pitch-up followed by a locked-in deep stall (see Chap. 9). Normally the stick shaker and pusher preclude this hazard; but a sudden strong downdraft can quickly put you well below shaker speed, as the Boeing incident shows.

Some aircraft break clean at stall and the nose drops low. Then if a strong updraft is encountered, the airspeed will increase rapidly and pulling Gs to get the nose up at high altitude puts you into buffet. With the nose still down airspeed builds rapidly; with Mach number exceeding M_{mo} you encounter shock induced flow separation and recovery becomes questionable. Flying too fast into moderate or severe turbulence can quickly put the aircraft into these high Mach hazards.

Stabilizer Drive Stall

Stabilizer drive stall is another possibility in either the turbulence upset accidents or runaway nose-down trim demonstrations. High indicated airspeeds make this most critical. If you enter a strong updraft and begin trimming the stabilizer nose down to resist the pitch and altitude change, you will be badly mistrimmed if the gust reverses. This reversal will naturally be opposed by elevator, which in turn loads the stabilizer—possibly enough to stall the trim drive. The elevator is unfortunately not large enough to fight both the gust and stabilizer. Later model jets have more powerful trim motors, but drive stall is still possible with enough airspeed.

Sonderlind (1963) writes regarding the Boeing 720B that "four units of stabilizer trim are roughly equivalent to full elevator. Get four units out of trim and all the elevator goes just to fight the stabilizer—none is left to recover from a dive or other unwanted maneuvers."

Now consider the runaway nose-down trim simulations at high speeds from around 16,000 ft, where shock induced flow separation is no longer involved. Two factors are important with cable and pulley flight controls. The first is a very high elevator force when pull-out is attempted. The elevator may seem immovable after V_{mo} is inadvertently exceeded. An increasing stick force is inherent to the system and helps prevent overstress by an apprehensive pilot, even in light airplanes. For example, it may take 60 lb of pull to provide a 2 G recovery at 250 KIAS but 200 lb at 425 K. And with nose-down trim applied the pull force required would be even greater.

In the NTSB mistrim evaluation of a Mark II Learjet (simulating the Vickery, Ohio, accident), spoilers were extended at V_{mo} with full nose-down trim. The elevator force needed to maintain level flight was estimated at between 120 lb and 140 lb. At 250 K it was measured at 98 lb. The 18 lb pull of the stick puller is obviously insignificant.

The second factor involved in high-airspeed dive recovery is stretch in elevator cables when very high aft control wheel pressure is applied. These two factors can combine to prevent elevator deflection and hence recovery.

Flutter and G Limitations

A pilot who inadvertently rolls nearly inverted during climb-out and then attempts to recover by "pulling through" (as in the Sabreliner mishaps mentioned early in this chapter) is not only certain to exceed V_{mo} but is very likely to encounter control surface flutter, which in itself can mean disaster. A BH125 crashed after the pilot experienced vertigo and unusual attitudes at night following a flight director failure over McLean, Virginia. It showed evidence of aerodynamic flutter before breakup.

The basic problem, however, involves the structural G limit and available altitude. A wing-over maneuver from approximately 18,000 ft at 260 KIAS would result in an airspeed buildup too great, even with idle power and drag devices, to recover successfully at the 3 G limit (see Fig. 5-13). NTSB reports on these types of accidents frequently show that the elevators separated before impact; as the ground got closer the pilot pulled harder until the structural limit was exceeded.

Student actions in a variety of high performance aircraft indicate that at altitude most pilots seldom pull very close to the available G limit in a dive

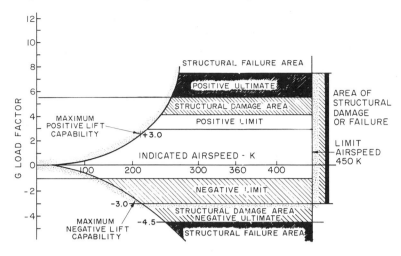

FIG. 5-13. Flight strength envelope of typical corporate jet.

recovery, even though they're trying. They usually lack aerobatic experience and greatly underestimate the allowable G force. Then in a pinch, when their proximity to the ground becomes obvious, they react in panic and either overstress the aircraft or, as in the cases mentioned, pull off one or both elevators.

Autopilot in Turbulence

Unless the manufacturer says differently, the autopilot *should be used* in moderate to severe turbulence. Naturally, the soft ride function should be selected if available. An overstress is not possible because its force is limited whereas the pilot's forces are not. Also, the autopilot (if it remains engaged) won't have instrument readability problems; nor will it be distracted by hail, lightning, or floating NAV charts and papers. Besides, use of the autopilot allows the pilot to monitor the instruments, which is also a safety factor. If it is too rough for the autopilot, make certain that yaw dampers remain engaged or Dutch roll (coupled roll and pitch oscillations) will become a problem.

Points to Remember

These points are important to remember when flying any jet aircraft:

1. Recommended or normal cruise is accomplished at the wing M_{crit} and provides the best compromise between a high true airspeed and best nautical miles per pound of fuel.

2. Cruising or descending faster than recommended by the manufacturer's charts can put you into drag divergence, which wastes fuel. Control surface buzz and Mach tuck may also occur.

3. Cruising or descending faster than M_{mo}, is dangerous because of shock induced flow separation and Mach tuck.

4. Don't try to climb above the normal cruise ceiling for gross weight and temperature aloft because it puts you too close to the low-speed buffet boundary if turbulence is encountered.

5. Moderate to severe turbulence encountered at FL 390 and above can quickly expose you to the hazards of both high-speed and low-speed buffet boundaries. The higher you go the more critical they are.

6. Know and abide by the turbulence penetration speed of your airplane. It's more important than you may think.

7. Learn the approximate thrust level (RPM) and the degree of nose-up pitch trim for your airplane at the turbulence penetration speed. Then, if you inadvertently encounter severe turbulence, you can establish an approximate attitude, approximate trim, and approximate power setting.

8. When moderate to severe turbulence is encountered, try to maintain the pitch attitude. The true airspeed will be adequate if thrust is set properly and a reasonably constant pitch attitude is maintained. Don't let large airspeed and altitude fluctuations tempt you to make large thrust or pitch trim changes. Engine compressor stall or flameout is also possible.

9. To avoid the buffet boundary in turbulence, maintain pitch attitude loosely. Use small to moderate elevator movements to oppose an attitude change. Above all do not try to rigidly hold altitude.

10. Use the autopilot if possible and by all means use the yaw damper.

Many pilots have flown many hours at high altitudes, but not all are educated to the aerodynamic factors involved. As the accident record shows, the air, like the sea, can be very unforgiving of ignorance. Because what you don't know can and will kill you.

6

Cruise Control

... OBTAINING BEST SPEED AND ECONOMY

THE ENERGY SHORTAGE has caused great concern in the world of general aviation. In the early seventies cruise control became a subject of major importance. Until fuel costs skyrocketed, most pilots were flying props and jets at maximum cruise speeds without much thought to economy. But rising fuel prices have caused a preoccupation with maximizing range—getting the most nautical miles per pound of fuel. Yet many pilots fail to consider all the aerodynamic facts involved.

The best angle of attack or long-range cruise speed in a jet or turbo prop is not always the most economical. In aircraft having nonturbocharged reciprocating engines, that long laborious climb to a high altitude is not usually economical unless you pick up strong tail winds. Conversely, with turbocharging, a climb to high altitude will increase cruise speeds and range somewhat. The principal advantage of a high altitude is the utilization of favorable winds aloft and avoidance of some weather. The pilot who moves from reciprocating engines to turbine power (turboprops and turbojets) finds a dramatic difference in cruise techniques.

Recips

Range and true airspeed (TAS) of a nonturbocharged reciprocating engine aircraft are not improved significantly with altitude because an extended climb at a high power setting, with attendant high fuel consumption (and engine wear), yields a slow true airspeed. Once you reach cruise level and use a specific horsepower, say 65%, you will find an insignificant difference in TAS and fuel flow compared to those at lower altitudes. The fuel flow (lb/hr) at 10,000 ft is almost identical to the fuel flow at 5000 ft (see Fig. 6-1).

A turbocharged engine however can climb high enough to realize additional range and a somewhat improved TAS. Also, the turbo engine's rated

CRUISE PERFORMANCE WITH RECOMMENDED LEAN MIXTURE AT 2500 FT

RPM	MP	%BHP	TAS	Total Lbs./Hr.	Endurance 600 Lbs.	Range 600 Lbs.	Endurance 978 Lbs.	Range 978 Lbs.	Endurance 1218 Lbs.	Range 1218 Lbs.
2450	24	74	208	168	3.57	743	5.82	1211	7.25	1508
	23	70	204	158	3.80	773	6.19	1260	7.71	1570
	22	66	198	147	4.08	810	6.65	1320	8.29	1644
	21	62	193	139	4.32	830	7.04	1358	8.76	1691
2300	24	68	201	153	3.92	789	6.39	1287	7.96	1603
	23	64	196	143	4.20	821	6.84	1338	8.52	1667
	22	60	190	135	4.44	846	7.24	1379	9.02	1718
	21	56	184	127	4.72	871	7.70	1421	9.59	1769
2200	23	58	187	131	4.58	859	7.47	1400	9.30	1743
	22	55	182	124	4.84	881	7.89	1436	9.82	1789
	21	50	174	116	4.17	899	8.43	1465	10.50	1825
	20	47	168	110	5.45	917	8.89	1495	11.07	1861
2100	22	49	172	113	5.31	914	8.65	1490	10.78	1856
	21	46	166	107	5.61	931	9.14	1517	11.38	1890
	20	43	158	101	5.94	940	9.68	1532	12.06	1908
	19	40	151	97	6.19	934	10.08	1522	12.56	1896
	18	37	139	90	6.67	923	10.87	1505	13.53	1874

CRUISE PERFORMANCE IS BASED ON STANDARD CONDITIONS, ZERO WIND, (50° F) RECOMMENDED LEAN MIXTURE, 600, 978 AND 1218 LBS. OF FUEL (NO RESERVE), AND 5300 POUNDS GROSS WEIGHT.

NOTE: See Range Profile, Figure 6-11, for range including climb.

CRUISE PERFORMANCE WITH RECOMMENDED LEAN MIXTURE AT 5000 FT

RPM	MP	%BHP	TAS	Total Lbs./Hr	Endurance 600 Lbs.	Range 600 Lbs.	Endurance 978 Lbs.	Range 978 Lbs.	Endurance 1218 Lbs.	Range 1218 Lbs.
2450	24	77	217	174	3.45	747	5.62	1217	7.00	1516
	23	73	212	164	3.66	774	5.96	1262	7.43	1572
	22	68	205	154	3.90	800	6.35	1303	7.91	1623
	21	64	200	145	4.14	827	6.74	1348	8.40	1678
2300	24	70	208	157	3.82	794	6.23	1295	7.76	1613
	23	66	202	148	4.05	819	6.61	1335	8.23	1662
	22	62	197	139	4.32	851	7.04	1387	8.76	1727
	21	58	191	131	4.60	876	7.47	1427	9.30	1778
2200	23	61	196	136	4.41	862	7.19	1406	8.96	1751
	22	57	189	128	4.69	886	7.64	1445	9.52	1799
	21	53	183	121	4.96	906	8.08	1478	10.07	1840
	20	50	177	115	5.22	923	8.50	1504	10.59	1874
2100	22	51	179	118	5.08	909	8.29	1482	10.32	1846
	21	48	173	111	5.41	935	8.81	1523	10.97	1897
	20	45	166	106	5.66	942	9.23	1535	11.49	1912
	19	42	157	99	6.06	951	9.88	1551	12.30	1932
	18	39	147	94	6.38	935	10.40	1524	12.96	1898

CRUISE PERFORMANCE IS BASED ON STANDARD CONDITIONS, ZERO WIND, (41° F) RECOMMENDED LEAN MIXTURE, 600, 978 AND 1218 LBS. OF FUEL (NO RESERVE), AND 5300 POUNDS GROSS WEIGHT.

NOTE: See Range Profile, Figure 6-11, for range including climb.

FIG. 6-1. Cruise performance at 2500 ft, 5000 ft, 7500 ft, and 10,000 ft.

horsepower does not diminish with altitude. Therefore the rate of climb remains constant and the average TAS during climb increases. Figure 6-2 shows that the Cessna 340A charts reflect a modest 25 K increase in cruise speed at 20,000 ft over 5000 ft. While this improvement is not great, the tail winds aloft can make a higher altitude worth the effort. If head winds are present a lower altitude is generally better.

Because TAS increases with altitude in turbocharged aircraft, a lower

CRUISE PERFORMANCE WITH RECOMMENDED LEAN MIXTURE AT 7500 FT

RPM	MP	%BHP	TAS	Total Lbs./Hr	Endurance 600 Lbs.	Range 600 Lbs.	Endurance 978 Lbs.	Range 978 Lbs.	Endurance 1218 Lbs.	Range 1218 Lbs.
2450	22	71	214	159	3.77	807	6.15	1315	7.66	1638
	21	67	208	150	4.00	833	6.52	1357	8.12	1691
	20	63	203	141	4.26	862	6.94	1405	8.64	1750
	19	58	195	132	4.55	888	7.41	1451	9.23	1807
2300	22	64	204	144	4.17	851	6.79	1388	8.46	1728
	21	60	198	136	4.41	874	7.19	1425	8.96	1774
	20	56	191	127	4.72	904	7.70	1474	9.59	1836
	19	53	186	121	4.96	921	8.08	1502	10.07	1870
2200	22	58	195	132	4.55	885	7.41	1443	9.23	1797
	21	55	190	126	4.76	903	7.76	1472	9.67	1834
	20	52	184	119	5.04	928	8.22	1513	10.24	1884
	19	48	176	112	5.36	941	8.73	1534	10.88	1911
2100	21	50	180	115	5.22	940	8.50	1532	10.59	1909
	20	47	173	110	5.45	943	8.89	1537	11.07	1914
	19	44	166	101	5.94	984	9.68	1604	12.06	1997
	18	40	152	97	6.19	939	10.08	1535	12.56	1911

CRUISE PERFORMANCE IS BASED ON STANDARD CONDITIONS, ZERO WIND, (32° F) RECOMMENDED LEAN MIXTURE, 600, 978 AND 1218 LBS. OF FUEL (NO RESERVE) AND 5300 POUNDS GROSS WEIGHT.

NOTE: See Range Profile, Figure 6-11, for range including climb.

CRUISE PERFORMANCE WITH RECOMMENDED LEAN MIXTURE AT 10,000 FT

RPM	MP	% BHP	TAS	Total Lbs./Hr	Endurance 600 Lbs.	Range 600 Lbs.	Endurance 978 Lbs.	Range 978 Lbs	Endurance 1218 Lbs.	Range 1218 Lbs.
2450	20	65	210	147	4.08	856	6.65	1395	8.29	1738
	19	61	204	137	4.38	892	7.14	1454	8.89	1811
	18	57	197	129	4.65	915	7.58	1491	9.44	1857
	17	53	189	121	4.96	937	8.08	1528	10.07	1904
2300	20	59	200	133	4.51	903	7.35	1472	9.16	1833
	19	55	193	125	4.80	927	7.82	1512	9.74	1883
	18	51	185	117	5.13	949	8.36	1546	10.41	1926
	17	48	178	111	5.41	961	8.81	1567	10.97	1951
2200	20	54	191	123	4.88	934	7.95	1522	9.90	1895
	19	50	183	116	5.17	945	8.43	1540	10.50	1918
	18	47	175	109	5.50	964	8.97	1571	11.17	1957
	17	44	159	104	5.77	920	9.40	1499	11.71	1867
2100	20	49	180	113	5.31	958	8.65	1561	10.78	1944
	19	46	172	107	5.61	963	9.14	1569	11.38	1954
	18	43	162	102	5.88	955	9.59	1556	11.94	1938
	17	40	140	96	6.25	873	10.19	1422	12.69	1771

CRUISE PERFORMANCE IS BASED ON STANDARD CONDITIONS, ZERO WIND. (23° F) RECOMMENDED LEAN MIXTURE, 600, 978 AND 1218 LBS. OF FUEL (NO RESERVE). AND 5300 POUNDS GROSS WEIGHT.

NOTE: See Range Profile, Figure 6-11, for range including climb.

cruise horsepower can be used to decrease fuel consumption and increase engine life. For example, the Cessna 340A cruising at 20,000 ft (standard temperature) pulling 75.2% HP provides 213 KTAS with a fuel flow of 204 lb/hr. But at 66.1% HP, TAS is 201 K with a fuel consumption rate of 181 lb/hr. On a 500 NM trip the flight time using 75.2% HP would be 2 hr 21 min, with 480 lb of fuel consumed. Flying at 66.1% HP, trip time is 2 hr 30 min and requires only 452 lb of fuel. At $1.95/gal the 5 gal saved means $9.75 less

SEA LEVEL / 5000 FEET

ALTITUDE	RPM	MP	−5°C (23°F) %BHP	KTAS	LB/HR	15°C (STD TEMP) (59°F) %BHP	KTAS	LB/HR	35°C (95°F) %BHP	KTAS	LB/HR
SEA LEVEL	2450	31.5	79.5	177	215	74.8	177	204	70.2	176	192
	2450	30.0	75.5	173	205	71.1	173	194	66.7	172	182
	2450	28.0	69.9	168	191	65.8	168	180	61.7	167	170
	2450	26.0	63.9	163	175	60.2	162	166	56.4	161	157
	2450	24.0	57.6	156	160	54.3	155	152	50.9	153	144
	2300	34.0	79.8	177	216	75.2	177	204	70.5	176	192
	2300	32.0	75.2	173	204	70.8	173	193	66.4	172	182
	2300	30.0	70.2	169	192	66.1	168	181	62.0	167	171
	2300	28.0	65.2	164	179	61.4	163	169	57.6	162	160
	2300	26.0	59.6	158	165	56.1	157	157	52.6	156	148
	2300	24.0	53.7	151	151	50.5	150	143	47.4	148	135
	2200	34.0	74.8	173	204	70.5	173	192	66.1	172	181
	2200	32.0	70.5	169	192	66.4	169	182	62.3	168	172
	2200	30.0	65.9	165	180	62.1	164	171	58.2	163	162
	2200	28.0	60.9	160	168	57.4	159	160	53.8	157	151
	2200	26.0	55.6	154	156	52.4	153	148	49.1	150	140
	2200	24.0	50.3	147	143	47.4	145	135	44.5	143	128
	2100	31.5	64.2	163	176	60.5	162	167	56.7	161	158
	2100	30.0	60.9	160	168	57.4	159	160	53.8	157	151
	2100	28.0	56.3	154	157	53.0	153	149	49.7	151	141
	2100	26.0	51.3	148	145	48.3	147	138	45.3	144	130
	2100	24.0	46.4	141	133	43.7	139	126	40.9	136	118

ALTITUDE	RPM	MP	−15°C (50°F) %BHP	KTAS	LB/HR	5°C (STD TEMP) (41°F) %BHP	KTAS	LB/HR	25°C (77°F) %BHP	KTAS	LB/HR
5000 FEET	2450	31.5	79.5	185	215	74.8	181	204	70.2	184	192
	2450	30.0	75.5	182	205	71.1	176	194	66.7	180	182
	2450	28.0	69.9	176	191	65.8	169	180	61.7	174	170
	2450	26.0	63.9	170	175	60.2	162	166	56.4	167	157
	2450	24.0	57.6	162	160	54.3	156	152	50.9	159	144
	2300	34.0	79.8	185	216	75.2	181	204	70.5	184	192
	2300	32.0	75.2	181	204	70.8	177	193	66.4	180	182
	2300	30.0	70.2	176	192	66.1	171	181	62.0	175	171
	2300	28.0	65.2	171	179	61.4	164	169	57.6	169	160
	2300	26.0	59.6	165	165	56.1	156	157	52.6	163	148
	2300	24.0	53.7	157	151	50.5	152	143	47.4	156	135
	2200	34.0	74.8	181	204	70.5	181	192	66.1	180	181
	2200	32.0	70.5	177	192	66.4	176	182	62.3	175	172
	2200	30.0	65.9	172	180	62.1	171	171	58.2	170	162
	2200	28.0	60.9	166	168	57.4	166	160	53.8	163	151
	2200	26.0	55.6	160	156	52.4	159	148	49.1	156	140
	2200	24.0	50.3	153	143	47.4	152	135	44.5	147	128
	2100	31.5	64.2	170	176	60.5	169	167	56.7	168	158
	2100	30.0	60.9	166	168	57.4	166	160	53.8	163	151
	2100	28.0	56.3	161	157	53.0	159	149	49.7	156	141
	2100	26.0	51.3	154	145	48.3	152	138	45.3	149	130
	2100	24.0	46.4	145	133	43.7	145	126	40.9	140	—

NOTE:
1. At Sea Level, increase speed by 2 KTAS for each 500 pounds below 5990 pounds.
2. At 5000 feet, increase speed by 2 KTAS for each 500 pounds below 5990 pounds.
3. Operations at peak EGT may be utilized with power settings within the boxes if the airplane is equipped with the optional EGT system.

20,000 FEET / 25,000 FEET

ALTITUDE	RPM	MP	−45°C (−48°F) %BHP	KTAS	LB/HR	−25°C (STD TEMP) (−12°F) %BHP	KTAS	LB/HR	−5°C (24°F) %BHP	KTAS	LB/HR
20,000 FEET	2450	31.5	79.5	213	215	74.8	213	204	70.2	211	192
	2450	30.0	75.5	209	205	71.1	208	194	66.7	206	182
	2450	28.0	69.9	202	191	65.8	200	180	61.7	197	170
	2450	26.0	63.9	193	175	60.2	191	166	56.4	188	157
	2450	24.0	57.6	183	160	54.3	180	152	50.9	175	144
	2300	34.0	79.8	214	216	75.2	213	204	70.5	211	192
	2300	32.0	75.2	208	204	70.8	208	193	66.4	205	182
	2300	30.0	70.2	202	192	66.1	201	181	62.0	198	171
	2300	28.0	65.2	195	179	61.4	193	169	57.6	190	160
	2300	26.0	59.6	186	165	56.1	184	157	52.6	180	148
	2300	24.0	53.7	176	151	50.5	172	143	47.4	165	135
	2200	34.0	74.8	208	204	70.5	207	192	66.1	205	181
	2200	32.0	70.5	203	192	66.4	201	182	62.3	198	172
	2200	30.0	65.9	196	180	62.1	194	171	58.2	191	162
	2200	28.0	60.9	189	168	57.4	186	160	53.8	182	151
	2200	26.0	55.6	180	156	52.4	177	148	49.1	170	140
	2200	24.0	50.3	170	143	47.4	164	135	44.5	154	128
	2100	31.5	64.2	194	176	60.5	192	167	56.7	188	158
	2100	30.0	60.9	189	168	57.4	186	160	53.8	182	151
	2100	28.0	56.3	181	157	53.0	178	149	49.7	172	141
	2100	26.0	51.3	172	145	48.3	167	138	45.3	157	130
	2100	24.0	46.4	160	133	43.7	152	126	40.9	129	118

ALTITUDE	RPM	MP	−54°C (−66°F) %BHP	KTAS	LB/HR	−34°C (STD TEMP) (−30°F) %BHP	KTAS	LB/HR	−14°C (6°F) %BHP	KTAS	LB/HR
25,000 FEET	2450	30.0	75.5	219	205	71.1	217	194	66.7	214	182
	2450	28.0	69.9	211	191	65.8	209	180	61.7	205	170
	2450	26.0	63.9	201	175	60.2	199	166	56.4	194	157
	2450	24.0	57.6	190	160	54.3	186	152	50.9	177	144
	2300	30.0	70.2	211	192	66.1	209	181	62.0	206	171
	2300	28.0	65.2	204	179	61.4	201	169	57.6	196	160
	2300	26.0	59.6	194	165	56.1	190	157	52.6	183	148
	2300	24.0	53.7	182	151	50.5	175	143	47.4	163	135
	2200	30.0	65.9	205	180	62.1	202	171	58.2	198	162
	2200	28.0	60.9	196	168	57.4	193	160	53.8	186	151
	2200	26.0	55.6	186	156	52.4	181	148	49.1	170	140
	2200	24.0	50.3	173	143	47.4	164	135	44.5	—	—
	2100	30.0	60.9	196	168	57.4	193	160	53.8	186	151
	2100	28.0	56.3	188	157	53.0	182	149	49.7	173	141
	2100	26.0	51.3	176	145	48.3	168	138	45.3	149	130
	2100	24.0	46.4	161	133	43.7	144	126	—	—	—

NOTE:
1. At 20,000 Feet, increase speed by 5 KTAS for each 500 pounds below 5990 pounds.
2. At 25,000 feet, increase speed by 6 KTAS for each 500 pounds below 5990 pounds.
3. Operations at peak EGT may be utilized with power settings within the boxes if the airplane is equipped with the optional EGT system.

FIG. 6-2. Cruise performance at sea level, 5000 ft, 20,000 ft, and 25,000 ft (*Cessna*).

cost/trip. Meanwhile the roughly 6% increase in trip time improved fuel consumption by 6%. If you flew this same trip once per month you would save $117 in fuel during the year.

Turbine Engines

Turbine engines (turboprops and turbojets) operate best in an environment quite different from that of reciprocating engines. First, turbine engines are more efficient at or near normal rated power. Second, the colder inlet temperatures at high altitude cause a significant reduction in specific fuel consumption (SFC). When these factors are combined with the large increase in TAS at very high altitudes, it is obvious why cruise at or above the tropopause is recommended.

Fan engines offer a slight exception to the rule. They too perform best at high altitudes, but FL 390 and FL 410 are not necessarily their magic numbers. In that rarefied atmosphere less ram air passes through the fan. Therefore in some aircraft the cruise charts show that above approximately FL 370 is a point where true airspeed diminishes. The peak or optimum altitude varies with temperature aloft and aircraft gross weight.

Altitude and Speed Limiting Factors

For turboprop and turbojet aircraft, gross weight and temperature aloft are the principal limiting factors to cruise altitude. Compressibility, which is a function of air density (altitude), is a limit to high-speed cruise.

Two methods are used to optimize fuel consumption and costs and to maximize range:

1. step climb from initial cruise altitude following fuel burn-off
2. constant altitude cruise, reducing thrust as gross weight diminishes with fuel burn-off, to maintain a target IAS or Mach number

Step climbing from the recommended initial cruise altitude in jet aircraft realizes a 2% range increase for every 2% weight reduction due to fuel burn-off. A step-climb is used for long-range flights. Cruise performance charts reflect the best initial cruise altitude for your gross weight at level-off and temperature aloft. So you must first get the temperature for altitudes you plan to use. If you forget to check temperature, then with a proposed cruise altitude above FL 310 I find that the temperature is generally ISA (International Standard Atmosphere) +10°C or 15°C (25°F). (See Fig. 6-3.)

Attempting to cruise above the optimum altitude for gross weight and temperature causes a loss in available range and TAS. It also increases the time at climb thrust, which increases engine hot section distress. Attempting to cruise at too high an altitude results in an excessive angle of attack with a resulting increased drag factor, which causes excesive fuel consumption. In the

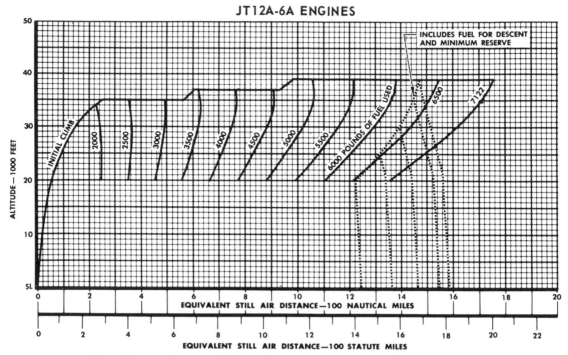

FIG. 6-3.   Effect of ISA + 25°F on climb and range (*Rockwell International*).

Sabre 60, for example, a climb to FL 370 following a maximum gross weight departure with temperature ISA +15°C aloft, the fuel flow at long-range cruise, .67M or 395 KTAS, will be closer to 2000 lb/hr than to the charted figure of 1540 lb/hr. Meanwhile at FL 350 or FL 330, a fuel flow of 2000 lb/hr will produce a cruise speed of 466 KTAS. Obviously the higher altitude is very uneconomical in both fuel and speed (Figs. 6-4 and 6-5).

Tailoring your fuel load to the specific trip keeps aircraft gross weight light and permits a higher initial cruise altitude. Therefore refueling should be delayed until cabin load, trip length, and destination weather are known. McDonnell Douglas says that for the DC9, 5000 lb of extra fuel increases the fuel used on a 300 NM trip by 2.9% and on an 800 NM flight by 7.1%.

Constant Altitude Cruise

Flying at a constant altitude is the usual procedure for short 1 or 2 hr flights. By reducing thrust and fuel flows to maintain recommended IAS or Mach number, then for every 2% reduction in gross weight due to fuel burn-off you will realize a 1% increase in range. Allowing IAS or Mach to increase with fuel burn-off reduces aircraft range and increases trip fuel costs.

As mentioned previously, temperature aloft is as important as the wind aloft. Warmer than ISA temperatures affect all aspects of cruise performance,

ZERO FUEL WEIGHT = 13,250 POUNDS, ISA + 15°C CONDITIONS, ZERO RESERVE

ALTITUDE	AVG MACH	KTAS	KIAS	FUEL FLOW RANGE LBS/HR
35,000	.651	388	221	1605 — 1180
37,000	.667	395	215	1540 — 1155
39,000	.676	401	213	1385 — 1135
41,000	.686	407	207	1240 — 1120

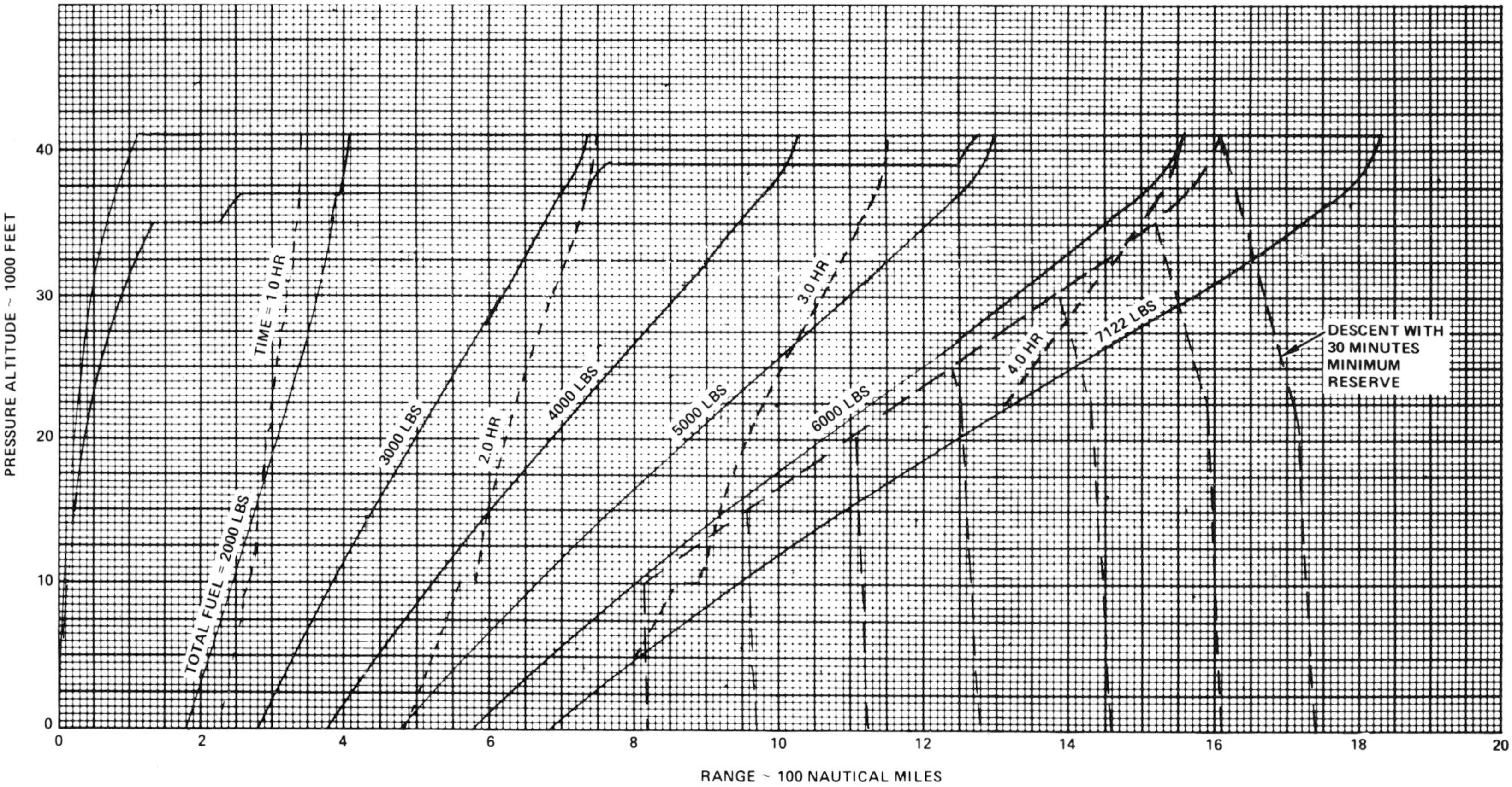

ALTITUDE	AVG MACH	KTAS	KIAS	FUEL FLOW RANGE LBS/HR
SEA LEVEL	.378	256	254	2665 — 2500
10,000	.468	307	263	2420 — 1955
20,000	.523	331	242	1975 — 1515
31,000	.614	370	227	1670 — 1240

FIG. 6-4. Cruise at maximum specific range versus altitude and fuel quantity (*Rockwell International*).

ZERO FUEL WEIGHT = 13,250 POUNDS, ISA + 15°C CONDITIONS, ZERO RESERVE

ALTITUDE	AVG MACH	KTAS	KIAS	FUEL FLOW RANGE LBS/HR
10,000	.638	418	361	3315 – 3215
20,000	.781	494	369	3350 – 3195
31,000	.800	484	302	2305 – 2180
33,000	.799	480	289	2135 – 2015

ALTITUDE	AVG MACH	KTAS	KIAS	FUEL FLOW RANGE LBS/HR
35,000	.797	475	276	1975 – 1867
37,000	.793	471	261	1790 – 1737
39,000	.786	466	248	1605 – 1580
41,000	.778	461	236	1430 – 1417

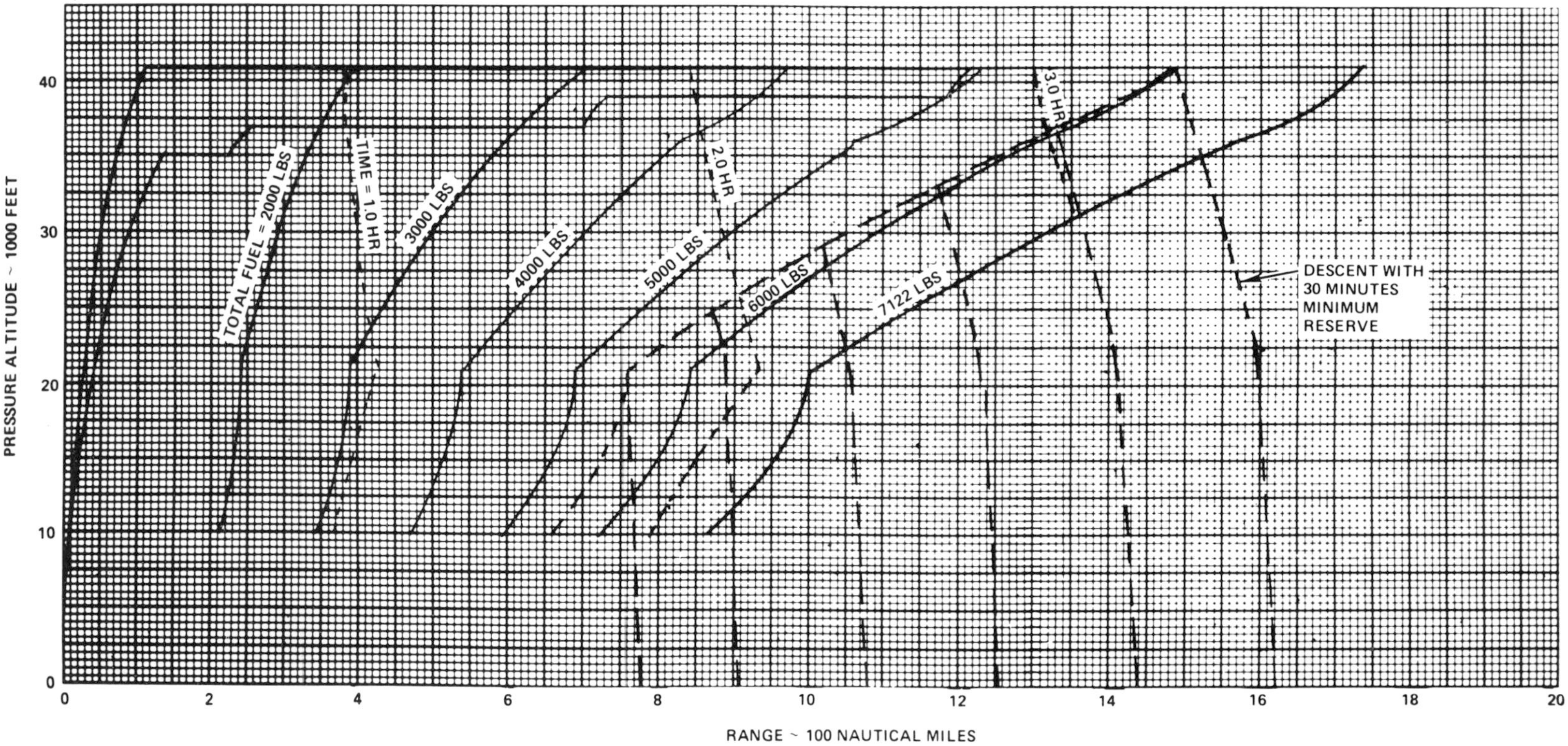

FIG. 6-5. Range at maximum speed cruise versus altitude and fuel quantity (*Rockwell International*).

beginning with attainable cruise altitude (based on gross weight) and including TAS, Mach number, fuel flow, EPR, and EGT (exhaust gas temperature) (see Fig. 6-6).

The effect of temperature on *range* is negligible when recommended or long-range cruise speeds are used. Engine EPR and EGT settings at these more fuel efficient speeds are generally well below maximum cruise thrust

ICAO STANDARD ATMOSPHERE TABLE

STANDARD S L CONDITIONS:
TEMPERATURE 15ºC (59ºF)
PRESSURE 29.921 IN. Hg 2116.216 LB/SQ FT
DENSITY .0023769 SLUGS/CU FT
SPEED OF SOUND 1116.14 FT/SEC 661.3 KNOTS

CONVERSION FACTORS:
1 IN. Hg = 70.727 LB/SQ FT
1 IN. Hg = 0.49116 LB/SQ IN.
1 KNOT = 1.151 MPH
1 KNOT = 1.688 FT/SEC

ALTITUDE FEET	DENSITY RATIO σ	$\dfrac{1}{\sqrt{\sigma}}$	TEMPERATURE ºF	TEMPERATURE ºC	SPEED OF SOUND (KNOTS)	PRESSURE IN. Hg
0	1.0000	1.000	59.0	15.0	661.3	29.92
1,000	.9711	1.015	55.4	13.0	659.0	28.86
2,000	.9428	1.030	51.9	11.0	656.7	27.82
3,000	.9151	1.045	48.3	9.0	654.4	26.82
4,000	.8881	1.061	44.7	7.0	652.1	25.84
5,000	.8617	1.077	41.2	5.1	649.8	24.90
6,000	.8359	1.094	37.6	3.1	647.5	23.98
7,000	.8106	1.111	34.0	1.1	645.2	23.09
8,000	.7860	1.128	30.5	− 0.9	642.9	22.22
9,000	.7620	1.146	26.9	− 2.9	640.5	21.39
10,000	.7385	1.164	23.3	− 4.9	638.1	20.58
11,000	.7155	1.182	19.8	− 6.8	635.8	19.79
12,000	.6932	1.201	16.2	− 8.8	633.4	19.03
13,000	.6713	1.221	12.6	− 10.8	631.1	18.29
14,000	.6500	1.240	9.1	− 12.8	628.7	17.58
15,000	.6292	1.261	5.5	− 14.8	626.3	16.89
16,000	.6090	1.281	1.9	− 16.8	623.9	16.22
17,000	.5892	1.303	− 1.6	− 18.7	621.4	15.57
18,000	.5699	1.325	− 5.2	− 20.7	619.0	14.94
19,000	.5511	1.347	− 8.8	− 22.7	616.6	14.34
20,000	.5328	1.370	− 12.3	− 24.6	614.1	13.75
21,000	.5150	1.393	− 15.9	− 26.6	611.7	13.18
22,000	.4976	1.418	− 19.5	− 28.6	609.2	12.64
23,000	.4807	1.442	− 23.0	− 30.6	606.8	12.11
24,000	.4642	1.468	− 26.6	− 32.6	604.3	11.60
25,000	.4481	1.494	− 30.2	− 34.6	601.8	11.10
26,000	.4325	1.521	− 33.7	− 36.5	599.3	10.63
27,000	.4173	1.548	− 37.3	− 38.5	596.8	10.17
28,000	.4025	1.576	− 40.9	− 40.5	594.2	9.725
29,000	.3881	1.605	− 44.4	− 42.5	591.7	9.297
30,000	.3741	1.635	− 48.0	− 44.5	589.2	8.885
31,000	.3605	1.666	− 51.6	− 46.5	586.6	8.488
32,000	.3473	1.697	− 55.1	− 48.4	584.0	8.106
33,000	.3345	1.729	− 58.7	− 50.4	581.5	7.737
34,000	.3220	1.762	− 62.3	− 52.4	578.9	7.382
35,000	.3099	1.796	− 65.8	− 54.4	576.3	7.041
36,000	.2981	1.832	− 69.4	− 56.4	573.6	6.712
37,000	.2844	1.875	− 69.7	− 56.5	573.4	6.397
38,000	.2710	1.921	− 69.7	− 56.5	573.4	6.097
39,000	.2583	1.968	− 69.7	− 56.5	573.4	5.811
40,000	.2462	2.015	− 69.7	− 56.5	573.4	5.538
41,000	.2346	2.065	− 69.7	− 56.5	573.4	5.278
42,000	.2236	2.115	− 69.7	− 56.5	573.4	5.030
43,000	.2131	2.166	− 69.7	− 56.5	573.4	4.794
44,000	.2031	2.219	− 69.7	− 56.5	573.4	4.569
45,000	.1936	2.273	− 69.7	− 56.5	573.4	4.355

FIG. 6-6. ICAO Standard Atmosphere Table. Tropopause begins at 36,086 ft; ISA temperatures at FL 310 and FL 350 are −46.5°C and −54.4°C, respectively (*Rockwell International*).

limits. Therefore when warmer than ISA temperatures are encountered you will note a slight drop in EPR, cruise Mach number, and IAS. When this occurs simply increase engine power (not to exceed maximum cruise thrust) to recover the lost EPR and airspeed. At first glance this would seem to increase fuel flow and thus reduce nautical miles per pound of fuel and aircraft range. But increased fuel flows are offset by an increase in TAS in the warmer, thinner air.

High altitude temperature limitations are reflected quite graphically in the Falcon 20F cruise charts (Fig. 6-7). Using ISA + 10°C and a modest gross weight of 25,000 lb, at maximum cruise thrust (maximum speed cruise) the Falcon 20F can climb to and cruise at FL 370 using Mach .703. The TAS is 410 K. If the pilot attempts to reach FL 390 at 25,000 lb (assuming ATC would allow a 2000 ft change), the chart shows that it can't be done. However after a

INDICATED MACH__TAS (kts)__EPR__FUEL FLOW (lbs/hr)__SPECIFIC DISTANCE (NM/lbs)

Pressure altitude : 37,000 ft

TEMP.	WEIGHT x 1,000 lbs	28	27	25	23	21	19
ISA − 10°C = − 66.5°C [RAT# − 45°C]	ind. M.	.738	.753	.771	.785	.796	.804
	TAS (kts)	410	418	428	435	441	446
	EPR	1.64	1.64	1.64	1.64	1.64	1.64
	F/F lbs/hr	980	990	1,005	1,015	1,020	1,025
	NM/lbs	.209	.211	.213	.215	.216	.217
ISA = − 56.5°C [RAT# − 35°C]	ind. M.		.713	.745	.763	.776	.786
	TAS (kts)		406	424	434	441	447
	EPR		1.62	1.61	1.60	1.60	1.60
	F/F lbs/hr		915	940	955	970	975
	NM/lbs		.222	225	.227	.228	.229
ISA + 10°C = − 46.5°C [RAT# − 25°C]	ind. M.			.703	.734	.752	.763
	TAS (kts)			410	427	438	444
	EPR			1.58	1.57	1.57	1.56
	F/F lbs/hr			855	880	895	905
	NM/lbs			.240	.242	.244	.245

39,000 ft

TEMP.	WEIGHT x 1,000 lbs	28	27	25	23	21	19
ISA − 10°C = − 66.5°C [RAT# − 42°C]	ind. M.			.733	.761	.777	.788
	TAS (kts)			408	423	432	438
	EPR			1.65	1.64	1.64	1.64
	F/F lbs/hr			890	910	925	930
	NM/lbs			.228	.232	.234	.235
ISA = − 56.5°C [RAT# − 32°C]	ind. M.			.675	.728	.754	.769
	TAS (kts)			385	415	429	438
	EPR			1.61	1.61	1.60	1.60
	F/F lbs/hr			800	847	870	882
	NM/lbs			.241	.245	.247	.248
ISA + 10°C = − 46.5° [RAT# − 25°C]	ind. M.				.662	.722	.745
	TAS (kts)				387	421	434
	EPR				1.58	1.57	1.56
	F/F lbs/hr				745	800	815
	NM/lbs				.259	.263	.266

Pressure altitude : 41,000 ft

TEMP.	WEIGHT x 1,000 lbs	28	27	25	23	21	19
ISA − 10°C = − 66.5°C [RAT# − 47°C]	ind. M.				.722	.753	.772
	TAS (kts)				402	419	429
	EPR				1.64	1.64	1.64
	F/F lbs/hr				815	835	845
	NM/lbs				.247	.251	.254
ISA = − 56.5°C [RAT# − 37°C]	ind. M.					.716	.747
	TAS (kts)					408	426
	EPR					1.61	1.60
	F/F lbs/hr					765	795
	NM/lbs					.266	.268
ISA + 10°C = − 46.5°C [RAT# − 27°C]	ind. M.						.706
	TAS (kts)						412
	EPR						1.57
	F/F lbs/hr						715
	NM/lbs						.288

FIG. 6-7. Maximum Cruise Thrust chart (*Falcon Jet*).

2000 lb fuel burn-off, the gross weight is reduced to 23,000 lb and the pilot can step climb to FL 390, *providing the temperature is ISA.*

Note however that if the temperature is again warmer than ISA the attainable cruise Mach is only .662 with TAS diminished to 387 K. Notice that these figures reflect a decreased TAS. It is therefore uneconomical in all respects—Mach, TAS, NM/lb fuel, fuel flow in lb/hr, and engine power (EPR/EGT)—to attempt cruise at FL 390. Not until gross weight diminishes to 21,000 lb in this warmer than ISA situation does this altitude become worthwhile. If however the temperature at FL 390 *is* ISA (−56.5°C), at 23,000 pounds you can cruise economically at .728M. Again this emphasizes the need to tailor fuel loads and keep takeoff gross weight as low as possible.

Turbojet Cruise Speeds

Three basic cruise speeds are reflected in the corporate jet flight manuals. First, *recommended cruise,* which at the tropopause is around Mach .75 for current generation aircraft (except for those with supercritical wings). On either side of recommended cruise are long-range cruise and maximum speed cruise. *Maximum or high-speed cruise* is generally the limiting Mach number (M_{mo}) and initially requires maximum cruise thrust. (The Falcon jet uses "maximum cruise thrust" to designate high-speed cruise.)

Long-range cruise provides 99% of the absolute maximum specific range or best nautical miles per pound of fuel. This 1% compromise in fuel flow results in a 3–5% higher cruise TAS (see Fig. 6-8). In a sampling of representative aircraft, this speed at the tropopause is Mach .69 to .7.

FIG. 6-8. Maximum Range Cruise Speed chart (*Rockwell International*).

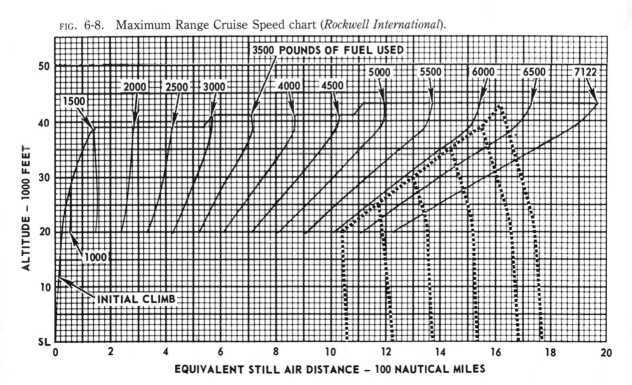

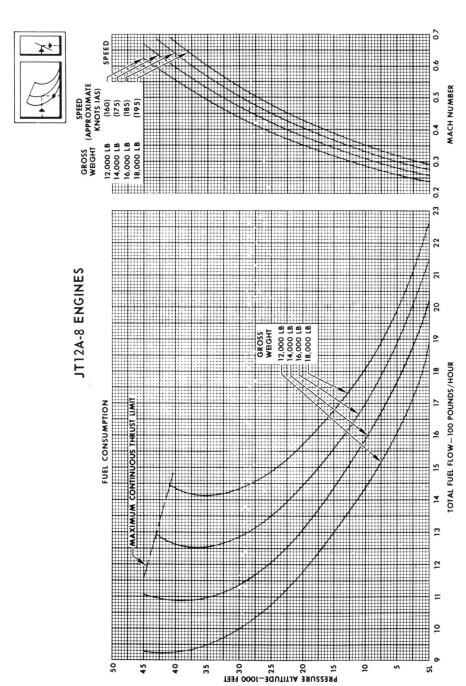

FIG. 6-9. Maximum Endurance chart (*Rockwell International*).

The Falcon 20F charts indicate best angle of attack, which changes with fuel burn-off. Cruising at best angle of attack or optimum range speed provides 100% best nautical miles per pound of fuel. However at high altitude the IAS is relatively slow so that constant thrust changes are required because of reduced speed stability, especially if turbulence is present.

Transport category aircraft have an additional chart for *maximum endurance* or loiter (Fig. 6-9) that provides maximum *flight time* per pound of fuel. The aerodynamic rule is that maximum endurance occurs at 75% of speed for maximum range cruise. It is useful primarily while holding. Unless antiice bleed air heat is required, holding should be done with flaps up. Extending approach flaps increases fuel consumption 2% or more.

Flying at maximum cruise speed without headwinds causes a degradation in nautical miles per pound; however, flight times are reduced. On a 1200 NM leg (no wind, climb, or descent figured) the charts show that for the aircraft sampled and cruising at 461 K (Mach .8, ISA temperature, FL 350), a crew would save 22 min over the long-range speed of 403 K (.7M). Based on Sabre 60 checklist charts, fuel consumed at the faster speed would be 5200 lb compared to 4650 lb at the slower long-range cruise. At recommended cruise the time saved would be a modest 13 min at Mach .74, with 4700 lb of fuel used. Obviously, at most altitudes recommended cruise is the best compromise between maximum speed and long-range cruise.

Turbojet Best Cruise Speed

While recommended cruise is the best trade-off between speed and fuel, the best speed for a given trip varies with atmosphere conditions, i.e., temperatures and winds aloft, and height of the tropopause.

In the jet fleet the best cruise speed has been subject to great debate; some airlines opt for long-range cruise, while many corporate operators prefer maximum cruise speed. Most sweptwing corporate jets have a high-speed cruise of about Mach .8; the airliners, with a greater wing sweep of around 35°, have a long-range cruise of Mach .8. For example, the Boeing 707 has a long-range cruise at .8M with high-speed cruise going up to .86M. The small, fast Falcon 10, with its computer designed wing, can cruise at .85M once the gross weight is reduced by fuel burn-off. Its long-range cruise is .75M.

There is a point at which atmospheric conditions make high-speed cruise more economical than long-range cruise. The aerodynamic rule is that with a head wind greater than 25% of recommended cruise TAS, maximum speed cruise should be used. In other words, in most aircraft, it is more economical in both fuel and flying time to cruise faster than 425–430 K with a headwind greater than 105–110 K.

To evaluate this head wind rule let's examine seven corporate aircraft; four varieties of the Sabreliner, the Lear 24B, the Falcon 20F, and the Jet Star with JT12-8 engines. With an enroute leg of 1200 NM and bucking a 110 K head wind at FL 350 and ISA conditions, here's how they looked.

The Sabre 40 with JT12A-6 engines and the Sabre 80 with CF 700-2D2 engines followed the rule perfectly. Using long-range cruise, flight time for the Sabre 40 was 4 hr 41 min with 6080 lb of fuel consumed; at maximum speed cruise flight time was 3 hr 39 min with 6030 lb of fuel used. At long-range cruise the Sabre 80 flew 4 hr 22 min over the 1200 NM course and burned 7080 lb; at maximum speed cruise it required only 3 hr 24 min and 7035 lb of fuel (IFR reserves not included).

The Sabre 80 saved 58 min of flying time and about 6 gal fuel. The Sabre 40 saved 63 min and 7 gal fuel. Considering the fixed cost per flying hour and the desire to fly at jet speeds, this saving is significant.

The saving in flying time of the other aircraft was equally impressive, although maximum cruise speed fuel consumption at FL 350 was slightly higher; 6.7 gal more in the Sabre 60, 15 gal more in the Jet Star, 41 gal more in the Falcon 20, and 37 gal more in the Lear 24B. However, the Sabre 60 at FL 390 (a more logical mean altitude for the tropopause) with the 110 K head wind saved roughly 45 min of flying and used less fuel at maximum speed cruise.

Two notable exceptions were the Lear 24B and the Falcon 20. The Lear continued to save 23 min but burned 88 gal more fuel at Mach .81 cruise. The increased fuel consumption reflects the drag rise associated with cruise above the critical Mach number. The Falcon 20 showed a distinct point of diminishing returns in Mach and TAS at altitudes above FL 370, caused no doubt by the fanned engine and thrust-to-weight ratio.

For the majority of turbojet airplanes, optimum cruise altitude will occur at the tropopause once you are light enough to get there. And the altitude at which you reach the tropopause will vary with the seasons of the year. Only temperature aloft will provide the answer. The ISA scale shows the tropopause beginning at 36,086 ft, the point at which the temperature stabilizes (Fig. 6-4).

Modifying Cruise Altitude Based on Winds Aloft

Although we have stressed cruising at the airplane's optimum cruise altitude, occasionally the pilot should fly at a *lower than optimum* altitude to obtain a wind advantage and thus realize a fuel savings. Since ATC procedures require altitude changes to be made in 4000 ft increments, careful consideration must be given to the head wind component change.

In the DC9, for example, McDonnell Douglas recommends that a 20 K decrease in head wind must be possible before an altitude 4000 ft lower than optimum is used. In the lower route structure used on relatively short trips, an altitude 2000 ft lower than optimum would be justified if a 10 K decrease in head wind could be achieved. (The same factors apply to a tail wind.)

For the big three corporate jets (Falcon 20F, Lear 24 and Sabre 60), the numbers vary. For the Falcon 20F and the Sabre 60, descending 4000 ft below optimum cruise altitude would require a decrease in the head wind of 30 K. For the Lear 24F a 40-K decrease in the head wind is required before a fuel savings can be realized.

Climb

In their climb charts the manufacturers go to great lengths to ascertain the best trade-off between maximum rate of climb and best true airspeed. For the Sabreliner series it is 260 KIAS until intercepting Mach .69, usually about FL 290 (see Fig. 6-10). A few manufacturers have published a high-speed climb procedure to help corporate aircraft keep up with airline traffic in high density traffic areas. In the Sabreliner it is Mach .73; in the Falcon 10, Mach .75. The

CLIMB DATA

MAXIMUM CONTINUOUS THRUST
260 KNOTS 0.69 MACH
STANDARD ISA CONDITIONS
EQUIVALENT STILL AIR DISTANCE

GROSS WEIGHT BRAKE RELEASE POUNDS	SEA LEVEL TO ALTITUDE	DISTANCE NAUTICAL MILES	TIME TO CLIMB MINUTES	FUEL USED POUNDS
20,000	10,000	13	3	230
	20,000	32	6	480
	30,000	72	13	780
	37,000	117	19	980
	39,000	150	24	1095
19,000	10,000	12	3	215
	20,000	30	6	445
	30,000	66	12	725
	37,000	106	18	940
	39,000	127	21	1035
18,000	10,000	11	2	205
	20,000	28	6	420
	30,000	61	11	670
	37,000	88	16	860
	39,000	113	19	935
	41,000	146	23	1055
17,000	10,000	10	2	190
	20,000	26	5	390
	30,000	56	10	620
	37,000	87	15	785
	39,000	101	17	850
	41,000	125	20	940
16,000	10,000	9	2	175
	20,000	24	5	360
	30,000	51	9	575
	37,000	79	13	715
	39,000	91	15	775
	41,000	109	18	840
	43,000	137	22	935

3C6-CL6-4A

FIG. 6-10. Climb Data chart (*Rockwell International*).

Mach .73 or .75 cruise climb is also effective against very strong head winds. Climbing faster than the manufacturer's recommended IAS or Mach number results in excessive fuel consumption and shortens aircraft range considerably.

As for climb winds, a good rule of thumb is to use 50% of the wind velocity at cruise altitude.

Following level-off, engine power is set for cruise *after* the Mach number reads about 0.01 faster than desired cruise; for a Mach .75 cruise accelerate to Mach .76 and reduce power to the recommended fuel flow. Under no circumstances should airspeed be allowed to fall below the target figure; drag and fuel consumption increase considerably and a high power setting is required to accelerate back to the target figure.

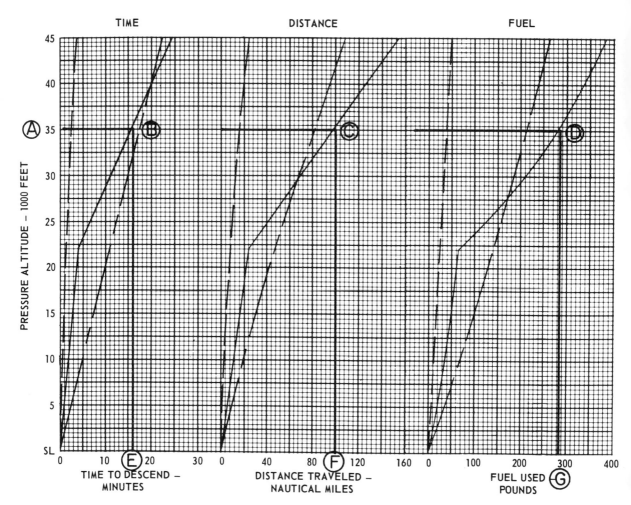

FIG. 6.11.   Descent data: standard ISA conditions (*Rockwell International*).

Descent Technique

The point to begin descent is a distance roughly (0.3 × FL) mi from your destination. At a cruise altitude of FL 350, under no-wind conditions you would begin descent 105 NM from your destination airfield or final approach fix. This calculation conforms to most aircraft descent charts—from jets to turboprops, light twins, and single engine aircraft. The technique often recommended is a modest power reduction with descent at a moderate Mach or IAS to an altitude at which idle power will maintain cabin pressurization.

For example, in the Sabre 60 descent is accomplished at .65M until intercepting 300 KIAS. Power is reduced slightly with an 1100 ft/min rate of descent maintained down to 22,000 ft. Below that altitude, if engine bleed air is not required for engine inlet antiicing, power is reduced to idle. Fuel consumed in a descent from FL 350 is about 285 lb (Fig. 6-11).

For the Sabre 80 with CF700-2D2 engines, Rockwell publishes a minimum RPM chart to ensure adequate pressurization. At FL 350 minimum RPM is about 78%. From 15,000 ft down, minimum RPM is 46% or idle. Again, as with the Sabre 60, descent is at .65M or 300 KIAS using 1100 ft/min rate of descent to FL 220. Below this level descent speed is 300 KIAS and rate of descent 4000 ft/min. For descent winds use 50% of the cruise altitude wind velocity.

As you can see, cruise control in a turbine engine airplane is quite involved. Because of time constraints in flight planning turboprop and turbojet operators can benefit greatly from a computer flight plan service. Because the computer automatically incorporates these factors into the cruise problem, the savings in fuel is considerably more than its annual cost. For this reason airlines have used computer flight planning since acquiring their first jets.

That High Altitude Environment

. . . KNOWING HOW TO SURVIVE

I T D O E S N ' T happen often but a sudden depressurization at altitude places you in a very hostile environment. You are, in effect, playing against time—seconds of useful consciousness; in 3–4 min irreparable brain damage or death occurs.

The five year statistics obtained from the FAA show 2500 pressurization problems. Not all were emergencies, but every type of aircraft has had a serious one. Older aircraft seemed the worst offenders, but new aircraft were involved in some instances. Sometime in 1979 a King Air 200 on a training flight in England experienced a pressurization failure or the flight instructor dumped the system. The aircraft later crashed in France with both pilots slumped over the control wheel. A Cessna 441 Conquest was similarly involved—at least that's the best guess. It climbed on autopilot to 41,000 ft, ran out of fuel, and crashed.

Perhaps the classic rapid decompression incident in a corporate type aircraft occurred on June 24, 1967. It involved an Air Force T-39A, forerunner of the Sabreliner 40. The investigation report stated that the aircraft was cruising at FL 450 in an effort to avoid thunderstorms. The copilot was wearing his helmet with the mask hanging loose by his face. The pilot was provided with a new (for that era) quick donning mask, which he elected to leave hanging beside the seat. The passengers were, fortunately, strapped in their seats.

Suddenly, with a cannonlike boom, the cabin door blew out, severely damaging the left engine and left horizontal stabilizer. The passengers and crew were instantly in a life or death situation. The copilot latched his mask and began pressure breathing. He later told investigators that when the fog cleared after the decompression, the pilot lay unconscious on the control wheel. The copilot immediately assumed command. With his left hand he held the pilot's body off the controls and with his right hand began an emergency descent.

During the emergency descent one of the passengers, who was also a pilot, at great personal risk came forward, using an emergency oxygen bottle. He stood by the gaping hole left by the door, and despite the suction created by the airflow, he pulled the pilot back in his seat and firmly planted an oxygen mask over the unconscious face. With oxygen under pressure now flowing into his lungs, the pilot began to revive; he was obviously affected by the worst possible form of decompression sickness, "central nervous system disorder." As he revived he became combative and began fighting wildly for control of the aircraft. It was theorized that some evolved gas (a nitrogen bubble) had stagnated at a critical point in his brain. Once again, despite his precarious foothold beside the open door of a jet executing an emergency descent, the passenger saved the day. According to the investigator's report, by wrestling with the pilot the passenger was able to restrain him and thus keep him off the flight controls.

Then, as if things weren't bad enough, one of the automatic (barometric) parachutes that AF regulations required for each occupant during that era deployed, filling the cabin with swirling silk. With frantic effort the remaining passengers prevented it from being sucked out of the door, where it would have hung up and affected elevator control. The left engine, though damaged and filled with debris from the cabin, continued to run at a low RPM, then finally flamed out. The copilot was unable to shut it down properly until just before landing, since he literally had his hands full.

After the flight landed safely at McConnell Air Force Base, an emergency medical team met the aircraft. Upon deplaning the still berserk pilot decked three of his benefactors. For three days he was restrained and in critical condition. In a last ditch effort to save his life the doctors placed him in a hyperbaric pressure chamber for compression therapy. Here the pressure was lowered to well below sea level; after the prescribed interval the evolved nitrogen was reabsorbed into his body fluids and he was returned to the hospital. Fortunately, thanks to his copilot, the passenger, and the medical team, he was physically and mentally normal and soon back to flight status.

The lesson is that there is a valid reason behind what many consider those "mickey mouse" regulations. In this instance the pilot was instantly incapacitated by hypoxia and bends. He did not have the hoped-for 5-8 s of useful consciousness in which to don his oxygen mask. This is why the quick-donning oxygen mask must be hung around the pilot's neck between FL 350 and FL 410.

Above FL 410, in most aircraft, both the crew and passengers must wear and use their masks. This requirement is found in the certificate limitations of the Airplane Flight Manual. The reason, as the T-39 incident shows, is that you may not be conscious enough to don your mask should decompression occur at extreme altitude.

Hypoxia

The pilot in the incident described suffered from hypoxia and what is commonly called *bends*. To understand hypoxia you must first understand what happens when we breathe air at sea level. Essentially gases always diffuse from areas of high pressure to areas of low pressure. The total pressure of a gas (air in this case) is equal to the sum of the partial pressures of the individual component gases of the mixture. Air inhaled into the lungs consists of 20% oxygen, 79% nitrogen, and 1% carbon dioxide and other gases. At sea level the total pressure of air is 760 mm Hg or 14.69 psi. Thus we could say that the partial pressure of oxygen is 20% of 760 mm Hg or 152 mm; nitrogen partial pressure would be 79% of 760 mm, or 600 mm.

When we inhale, air is pumped into tiny air sacs in the lungs called alveoli. The walls of the alveoli are filled with tiny vessels called capillaries. The pressure of inhaled air forces the oxygen and nitrogen through the alveoli capillary membrane (or alveoli wall) called septa and into solution with the blood. Meanwhile the blood returns carbon dioxide (CO_2) from the body tissue. The body balances these gases and the alveolar (larger division of air sac) air is maintained at a fairly even partial pressure of both gases. Diminishing the oxygen partial pressure by climbing to a higher atmospheric pressure causes oxygen deficiency, commonly called *hypoxia*.

Conversely, breathing too fast (hyperventilating) diminishes the CO_2 partial pressure and produces symptoms similar to hypoxia. Either condition leads to unconsciousness. Nitrogen is inert and maintained in equilibrium within the body.

Because of the mixing of gases in the lung and the necessary presence of water vapor, the total air pressure of 760 mm Hg in the lungs at normal body temperature (37°C) includes a partial pressure of CO_2 of 43 mm Hg (6%); water vapor, 47 mm; oxygen, 100 mm Hg; and nitrogen, 563 mm Hg. The remainder is composed of rare gases or a variance in the nitrogen partial pressure.

At sea level oxygen saturation of blood is 90–98%. If the alveolar partial pressure of oxygen decreases to less than 60 mm Hg the percent of blood saturation falls off rapidly. To prevent hypoxia and ensure normal functions the oxygen partial pressure must be maintained in a range of 60–100 mm Hg. At lower altitudes the addition of oxygen in proper proportions to the ambient air is adequate. However at 34,000 ft 100% oxygen is required to maintain the 100 mm Hg oxygen partial pressure. Above 34,000 ft, 100% oxygen under pressure must be provided if a sea level oxygen blood saturation is to be maintained. Otherwise it would decline so that at 40,000 ft the percent oxygen saturation in the lungs would be equivalent to ambient air at 10,000 ft.

Hypoxia Altitudes

Dissecting the T-39 accident, let's look first at the hypoxia aspect. A general misconception is prevalent that only jets get to altitudes where hypoxia can become a problem. Not so! The first signs can begin as low as 5000 ft (see Fig.

7-1) and can be demonstrated in the altitude chamber. At a chamber altitude of 5000 ft, with the lights off, the trainee is asked to watch a pattern of colored lights. After a given interval the trainee puts on the mask and takes a deep breath of 100% oxygen. The lights immediately become brighter. It is especially noticeable to a smoker since after a recent cigarette a smoker's effective altitude is 3000–5000 ft higher than nonsmoker's. The cells in the eye's retina that are used for low levels of illumination are extremely sensitive to hypoxia— at 12,000 ft, breathing ambient air, your eyes will lose about 25% of their effective night vision.

FAR 91.32 states that with a cabin altitude between 12,500 and 14,000 ft the crew must use oxygen for flights longer than 30 min, and above 14,000 ft the crew must use oxygen continuously. The passengers, of course, require oxygen above 15,000 ft. Here's why. At 14,000 ft the symptoms of hypoxia are forgetfulness and indifference. Higher, after approximately 30 min at 18,000 ft and without significant activity, the individual will be completely impaired. Any activity, such as going back to check the cargo, moving a bag, or getting a cup of coffee, will shorten this time considerably.

The real danger point is at FL 260 and above, where the alveolar partial pressure of oxygen is lower than the oxygen partial pressure of the blood. A sudden decompression at FL 260 results in a reverse flow of oxygen *out* of the blood and into the atmosphere. Consequently the onset of hypoxia is much more sudden and the time of useful consciousness (TUC) is shortened significantly. As a rule of thumb your time of useful consciousness is reduced by about 50%. Age, poor physical condition, and obesity also shorten TUC.

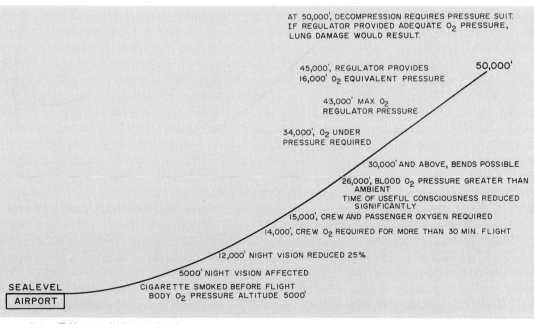

FIG. 7-1. Effects of high altitude.

Hyperventilation

Hyperventilation is usually the result of excitement, such as the thrill of a sudden explosive decompression when a door seal splits or a window blows out. This "overbreathing" actually produces a hypoxic condition of the brain. When the body senses a fall in the carbon dioxide level of the blood, the depth and rate of breathing increase, intensifying the problem.

My first experience occurred while I was testing an Air Force F105D. It was caused by an irritating, tight fitting mask. Because it was work to breathe against the regulator valves I had distorted my face so that air was coming in alongside my cheek. It was easier to breathe, but shortly my breathing rate increased and I became dizzy. Because of previous training in the altitude chamber I held my mask close, selected 100% oxygen, slowed my breathing rate (actually held my breath for a moment), and returned to breathing through the mask. Aborting the flight was a rather conservative move, but there had been numerous unexplained single pilot accidents in high performance aircraft over the years that could have been caused by hyperventilation.

The symptoms of hyperventilation are basically a shortness of breath followed by a feeling of dizziness. In my case the skin on my back and upper arms tingled. Some may have this sensation in fingers and toes.

Bends

A case of *bends* can be either painful or totally debilitating, as the T-39 incident shows. The technical term, *decompression sickness,* includes bends, chokes, central nervous system disturbances, and skin manifestations. The cause of decompression sickness is the commonly accepted nitrogen bubble theory. It is based on Henry's law, which states that the amount of gas that will dissolve in a solution (our body fluids) and remain in solution is directly related to the pressure of the gas (in this case the atmosphere) over the solution.

The primary gas involved in formation of bubbles in the body is the otherwise inert nitrogen. Ordinarily nitrogen pressure in the body is in equilibrium with the nitrogen pressure in the alveoli of the lungs. The pressure of nitrogen in the alveoli depends on the total barometric pressure. When the barometric pressure falls the alveoli nitrogen pressure diminishes and results in an imbalance of nitrogen pressures between the alveoli and blood. Then, according to the law of gas diffusion, the nitrogen in the blood will diffuse into the alveoli and be expelled during exhalation.

When the blood with the lowered nitrogen pressure recirculates it picks up higher pressure nitrogen from body tissues and returns it to the alveoli for exhalation. The body is attempting to keep the nitrogen pressure equalized throughout. The problem is that blood, a so-called fast phase tissue, releases its nitrogen rapidly. (Muscle or lean tissue expels nitrogen moderately fast and is called medium phase tissue; fat releases nitrogen very slowly and is a slow phase tissue. Therefore obese individuals are much more susceptible to decompression sickness.) During sudden decompression the pressure gradient between the atmosphere and body nitrogen pressure becomes so great that the dissolved body nitrogen "evolves" or comes out of solution before reaching the alveoli. This causes nitrogen bubble formation not only in the blood but in other body fluids and body tissues.

While a simple case of bends—pain that usually develops in or around the bony joints—may not be incapacitating, it is very important not to move the limb involved or try to work the pain out. Exercise, such as walking aft to assist a passenger who doesn't know how to get the oxygen started or can't get the mask on, not only spreads the pain but precipitates bends at a much lower altitude. The crew must be certain that the passengers understand how to use the oxygen system before departure, because with a rapid decompression the crew's sole concern is an emergency descent for everyone's sake. And both crewmembers are very busy.

Other factors relate to how fast and at what altitude you may experience decompression sickness. The older you are the more likely you are to experience bends. Obesity, or more correctly, ratio of weight to height has an important bearing on susceptibility.

It is generally accepted that 30,000 ft is the critical altitude for experiencing bends. However, documented cases of decompression sickness have occurred as low as 18,000 ft—decompression sickness is a function of individual susceptibility that can vary from day to day.

Another form of decompression sickness is *true chokes*. It's rare but dangerous and caused by bubbles in the smaller blood vessels of the lungs. Symptoms include a deep sharp pain under the breastbone, a dry progressive cough, and loss of ability to take a normal breath. The victim will begin to sense suffocation and symptoms of shock will develop.

The T-39 pilot had the most dangerous form of bends, *central nervous system disturbance*. This too is rare. The brain, and less frequently the spinal cord, is involved. While no particular behavior pattern develops, the usual symptoms are disturbances of vision such as blind spots or flickering lights.

Vasomotor and neurocirculatory collapse are other remote (serious) possibilities. If an individual goes into shock or collapses, either during or after a rapid decompression, you must promptly seek medical attention. If the condition persists, indicating the nitrogen bubbles are still present after the flight, compression therapy is required.

The symptoms of bends vary with individuals. Frequently the first symptom is a tingling sensation on the skin of the back and upper arms, called *paresthesia* or *creeps*. Then an ever increasing pain quickly develops in the elbows or knees. Symptoms of bends may vary from episode to episode; prolonged exposure can lead to shock and unconsciousness.

Breathing pure oxygen after bends develop will not give relief. To be effective this denitrogenation must be done for at least 30 min *before* exposure. After bends develop the only cure is to descend below the altitude at which the problem occurred. If the pain continues at ground level, compression therapy is needed, as the T-39 case illustrates.

Sinus and Ear Involvement

Other examples of trapped gases that can be exceedingly painful include blockage of the middle ear (barotitis media), sinuses (barsinusitis), barodontalgis (toothache with altitude), and/or tooth abscess. The two you are most likely to encounter, especially when flying with a cold, are middle ear blockage and a plugged sinus.

If you have a severe cold and fly an older turboprop or light twin at cruise altitude with cabin pressure of 10,000–11,000 ft (the altitude warning light will be on), on descent you will likely have an ear and sinus problem. With a plugged ear, a descent from 18,000 ft to sea level produces a pressure differential of half an atmosphere. Without pressure relief such as Valsalva (holding your nose and blowing gently to make the ears or sinus clear) you might suffer a ruptured eardrum. At the very least you'll have fluid or perhaps mucus forced into the middle ear that can result in a serious infection. A plugged sinus can close your eyes with pain. It can also cause more pain in certain teeth than an abscess. Again, unless the sinus block is cleared, the pain can drive a person wild. And the fluids forced into the sinus by increasing atmospheric pressure are a potential source for serious infection.

The lesson is: (1) don't fly with a severe cold, and (2) when you fly with some congestion make certain that you have good strong nose drops on board. In fact, nose drops and decongestant tablets should be part of your galley supplies for passengers (and crewmembers after the flight). A single pilot operator should be especially cautious because either of these conditions can incapacitate you and preclude a safe landing.

Oxygen Regulators

Three basic types of oxygen systems are (1) continuous flow, (2) diluter demand, and (3) pressure demand. The continuous flow system provides the user with a continuous flow of 100% oxygen. This system is good up to 25,000 ft or 30,000 ft in an emergency, according to the U.S. Air Force. It is provided for passengers and crew of less sophisticated aircraft. Some manufacturers using improved crew masks have FAA certification to 33,000 ft, which approaches the 34,000 ft changeover point from 100% oxygen to pressure oxygen (Fig. 7-2).

The more sophisticated diluter demand system (Fig. 7-3) is found on the more expensive aircraft—the King Air 200 and Citation I, to name two. The Air Force limits these regulators to a normal altitude of 35,000 ft or in an emergency to 40,000 ft. The improved system found on the Citation I is certified to 41,000 ft. The diluter demand system is designed to prevent even small amounts of ambient air from getting to the pilot's lungs in the higher altitude environment (i.e., above 34,000 ft). To conserve oxygen, it delivers oxygen on demand during inhalation. At lower altitudes this system automatically mixes oxygen with the ambient air.

The pressure demand oxygen system (Fig. 7-4) is designed to be used up to 50,000 ft in an emergency. Its normal ceiling in the Air Force is considered to be 43,000 ft, with emergency use above that level. The Air Force says that with standard pressure breathing equipment the blood oxygen saturation will be 76% at 45,000, which is equivalent to breathing air at 16,000 ft. Therefore a decompression above FL 430 requires an emergency descent. From sea level to 30,000 ft the pressure demand system with the selector on normal provides a mix of oxygen and ambient air, the same as the diluter demand system. Above 30,000 ft oxygen is supplied under pressure to force it into the blood stream.

A pilot recently told an assembled group of fellow aviators how he climbed his corporate jet to 47,000 ft, which was 2000 ft over its certified altitude. The manufacturer knows it can be done at light gross weights, but the aircraft is not certified to those heights, primarily because of the oxygen system.

The pressure demand oxygen regulator attempts to maintain an alveolar oxygen partial pressure at the sea level equivalent of 60–100 mm Hg. Up to 34,000 ft the regulator will maintain the proper oxygen mix to accomplish this task. Above 34,000 ft the regulator provides 100% oxygen under positive pressure to maintain a sea level equivalent in the lungs. The pressure begins gently at first, at about 3.7 mm Hg, then builds up to 31 mm Hg at 43,000 ft. Above 43,000 ft the regulator is limited to 31 mm Hg because the lung tissue can't take much more. A higher pressure causes the alveoli to stretch and press against the capillaries, impeding passage of red blood cells and plasma. At an oxygen pressure of 40 mm Hg the eardrums distend painfully and pressure breathing causes pain near the eyes. Lung damage becomes a distinct possibility.

FIG. 7-2. Continuous flow oxygen mask.

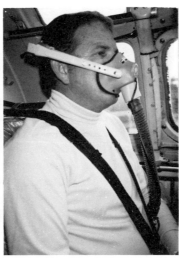

FIG. 7-3. "Horse collar" diluter demand oxygen mask.

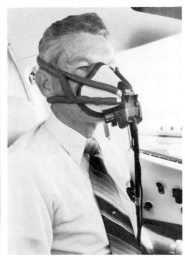

FIG. 7-4. Scott quick-don pressure demand oxygen mask.

Pressure breathing in itself requires special training in the altitude chamber. With a decompression at 43,000 ft or 45,000 ft the regulator fills your lungs with pressure oxygen and your mask must fit tightly to ensure that oxygen gets into your bloodstream. As a result you must forcefully exhale against the pressure. This is actually reverse breathing.

Later model Learjets, certified to 51,000 ft, have a specially stressed "pressure vessel" that passed the same rigorous certification test required of a supersonic transport. Because of this extra strength they retain the conventional pressure demand oxygen system.

Points to Remember

Remember the following points about the high altitude environment in which you fly.

1. The passengers must know how to fend for themselves should a sudden decompression occur. The crew can't help because each will be busy saving the airplane. Arrange a special seminar for your frequent passengers. Let them see the masks fall out; let them pull the pin that starts oxygen flow and reinsert the pin when oxygen is no longer needed. In the lower flying turboprop aircraft they must be able to locate the masks in the pocket behind the seat, insert the male prong into the oxygen receptacle, and begin breathing oxygen. This procedure can be time consuming and the physical effort required, coupled with fear, can lead to unconsciousness.

2. In fancier equipment with automatically deployed masks, the passengers must know to pull the pin to get the oxygen started. They must also understand that a lighted cigarette and a constant flow of oxygen equal disaster.

3. With the emergency portable oxygen bottle, the mask should be plugged in during preflight and the function switch set on normal because when you need it, you need it fast. After flight it should of course be turned off and the mask unplugged to prevent leakage. During training sessions, I have found emergency oxygen masks with the male prong too long to allow a connection. In some less sophisticated continuous flow systems, problems also develop with the cockpit oxygen plug, wherein the aircraft female connector needs lubrication and not just any lubricant will do. Remember that petroleum products and oxygen can make a fire faster than a boy scout.

4. If you experience a decompression get your mask on tightly and execute an emergency descent. In a jet be careful not to roll over so abruptly that you get the nose down too far and encounter Mach tuck.

5. After a decompression above FL 350, do not attempt to crawl back and help a passenger. The walk-around bottle mask will not fit tightly enough to support consciousness and, also, bends are a certainty. Get down to a lower altitude first.

6. Light twin and turboprop pilots should not fly at altitude with an oxygen cylinder empty. (This practice is common when the system develops a leak and the pilot does not understand the importance of oxygen at 18,000 ft to 25,000 ft.)

7. Above all visit the free FAA altitude chamber at Oklahoma City, or for a fee, schedule a visit at one of the Navy, Air Force, or Marine chambers spotted around the country. Your General Aviation District Office has the forms and the schedule.

8. Obey the regulations. They were born of the unhappy experiences of an earlier generation.

When Your Engine Coughs

. . . JET ENGINE COMPRESSOR STALLS

C O M P R E S S O R S T A L L S in modern turbine engines are relatively rare. Yet when they occur it is necessary for the pilot to take prompt corrective action or risk engine damage or total destruction. There are several possible causes; fuel control malfunction is a regular contributor and compressor damage due to ice ingestion or bird strike is another.

The most insidious situation the professional pilot faces routinely is an inadvertent encounter with thunderstorms in which compressor stalls can be precipitated by inlet airflow distortion, ingestion of large amounts of water and hail, or a combination of these factors complicated by erratic power management on the part of the frightened or at least apprehensive pilot. When misfortune puts you in the bowels of a thunderstorm even the bravest of souls experiences a sharp increase in "pucker factor." With the airspeed needle dancing wildly from the red line to below stall speed and the altimeter racing precipitously well above or below your assigned altitude, there is an instinctive reaction to increase or reduce power quickly as the situation appears to demand. Yet this is the worst thing a pilot can do.

The Southern Airlines DC9 crash at New Hope, Georgia, on April 4, 1977, provides a classic example of what can happen. The flight was cleared to descend from 17,000 ft to 14,000 ft. Although in heavy turbulence, rain, and hail for a number of minutes, the NTSB report theorized that the pilot flying reduced power to idle for the descent. This resulted in engine rollback (loss of RPM) to less than idle power because of rain and hail ingestion.

This procedural mistake is often overlooked in training. In heavy weather, especially at altitudes between 10,000 ft and 20,000 ft, you are consistently in an area of freezing temperatures combined with a high moisture content; therefore drag devices, such as speed brakes or spoilers, are required to control descent airspeed while power is maintained around 1.2–1.5 EPR (75–80% in most corporate jets) to provide adequate engine bleed air for antiicing. Subsequent tests revealed that had the DC9 crew followed this procedure, once the water content of the air diminished, engine rollback would have recovered to the thottle setting without surge or flameout. Instead, when the RPM loss occurred, the crew is thought to have advanced the power levers. This was borne out by survivors' statements concerning severe compressor stalls. Without training emphasis to the contrary, advancing throttles would be an instinctive reaction to an RPM rollback.

The engines were subsequently found with obvious evidence of overtemperature. In addition, the sixth-stage compressor blades had deflected forward and collided with the fifth-stage stator vanes; "pieces of vanes and blades were then ingested into the high pressure compressors causing extreme damage. . . ." Contrary to speculation no evidence of compressor damage due to hail was found. Therefore the board concluded that hail ingestion was not responsible for the compressor damage that resulted in double engine failure. Improper pilot technique caused the engines to fail *because the compressor stalls were not correctly resolved.*

Two recent Learjet incidents highlight the critical limits to engine operation at high altitude. In the most recent mishap the aircraft was flying at 45,000 ft in clear air. The autopilot malfunctioned in pitch and caused the angle of attack to increase suddenly though not violently. The engines were operating so close to their stall margin in that rarefied atmosphere that they both simultaneously flamed out. According to the report, the crew descended to 28,000 ft where they were able to obtain a relight.

A more spectacular accident occurred to an Air Force crew flying a T-39A. They were on a night proficiency flight in a nonradar equipped airplane. In an attempt to avoid thunderstorms and turbulence they climbed to FL 430. Unfortunately they could not top the weather. The turbulence increased with a sudden severe jolt, snuffing out both engines. They were forced to descend into the thunderstorm, which according to the accident report, had tornado activity, severe turbulence, heavy rain, and hail. All attempts to air-start the engines were unsuccessful. They reportedly used a flashlight to illuminate the powerless turn-and-slip indicator. (The T-39 does not have a standby attitude indicator and power pack.) Finally, after a terrorizing descent they broke out at 5000 ft. Using the illumination of lightning flashes they managed to touch down with gear extended on a highway, then ran off into a field where a telephone pole severed 3 ft from the right wing. After crossing a built-up highway the gear sheared and the nose dug into soft ground, finally halting the slide. All three crewmembers received serious injuries but no one was killed.

The Turbine Engine

In a simplified review of how a jet engine functions, let's begin with the air provided at the compressor inlet (Fig. 8-1). From the inlet the air is compressed, which adds energy in the form of pressure. This pressurized air is then ducted through an enlarged diffuser passage that reduces velocity somewhat and provides better combustion. In the combustion section fuel is injected and burned. The burning hot gases are then ducted through the turbine nozzle to the turbine wheels, which in turn drive the compressor.

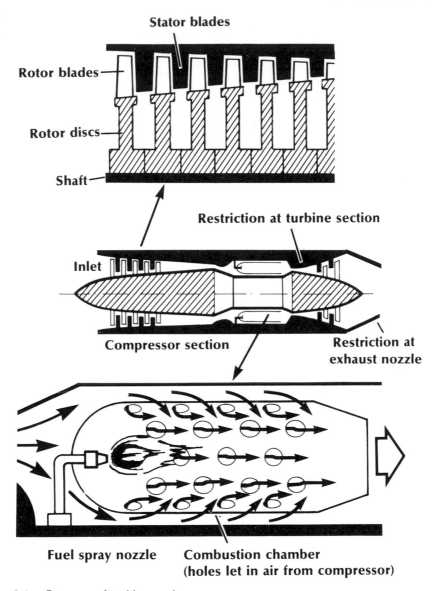

FIG. 8-1. Cutaway of turbine engine.

While the pressure drops only slightly from compressor through the combustion section, the velocity increases as air is forced around the forward end of the combustion section and through holes in the side of combustion chamber inner liners (Fig. 8-1). The airflow is again constricted as it encounters the converging partitions of the turbine nozzle, resulting in a sudden increase in air velocity. Approximately 75% of this velocity increase is used to drive the compressor. Farther aft these hot gases are once again constricted, this time by the exhaust nozzle. The exhaust gas velocity is again increased sharply, which results in the production of thrust.

The turboprop engine is slightly different. It converts most of the turbine section airflow into mechanical energy to drive the compressor and accessories. Consequently only a small amount of exhaust gas thrust is produced.

Not all the air passing through a turbine engine is used in combustion. Only about 1 lb of every 4 lb of air passed through is used for combustion. The unburned air is used to cool various hot section parts (combustors or fire cans) and contributes to thrust by providing increased mass to the exhaust.

Most turbine engines used in corporate jets and turboprops utilize axial flow compressors. The term *axial flow* is used because airflow and compression occur parallel to the rotational axis of the compressor. The Garrett TFE 731 and JT15D-4 Turbofan bypass engines are exceptions. The TFE 731 has a four stage low pressure axial flow compressor with a high pressure centrifugal compressor wheel. The JT15D-4 Turbofan in the Citation and Diamond I is similar but has only a compressor fan, one set of guide vanes, and a high-speed centrifugal compressor.

The axial-flow compressor is constructed on a conical-shaped rotor containing several rows of fanlike blades placed so that each blade directs air to the next one. The compressor rotor consists of a series of disks joined together with each one containing compressor blades mounted around its circumference. Between each row of compressor blades are the stators extending radially from the compressor case. They direct air from one stage to the next. Air compression is achieved by tapering the disks so that the largest diameter disk in the last stage has the smallest compressor blades (Fig. 8-1). This shaping results in air being forced into progressively smaller spaces as it is directed from stage to stage.

The airfoil-shaped compressor blades react much like wings in that their angle of attack to the incoming air produces a low pressure area above and a high pressure area below (Fig. 8-2). A compressor operating at its maximum design speed causes these blades to achieve an angle of attack very close to maximum (stall), which is the point of maximum pressure rise. And because

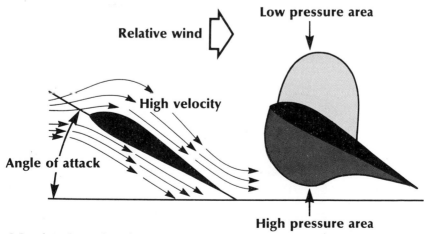

FIG. 8-2. Aerodynamics of compressor blades.

compressor blade angle is near maximum, the compressor is very close to its stall margin.

A primary consideration in engine design is *compression ratio,* a comparison between engine inlet air pressure and compressor discharge pressure. To determine how much thrust a new engine is capable of delivering, engineers must first know what compression ratio a compressor can maintain. At rated thrust output this compression ratio must exceed the back pressure created by restrictions to airflow in the hot section and turbine and exhaust nozzles.

Of more immediate concern to the pilot is engine pressure ratio (EPR), a comparison of the turbine discharge pressure and engine inlet pressure. The EPR gage gives the crew a direct reading of engine power or thrust output. For takeoff a static EPR requirement of 2.24 (as obtained from the checklist chart) means turbine discharge pressure relative to compressor inlet pressure is 2.24 to 1. Anything less than this is less than maximum power. A slow power application during a rolling takeoff may result in achieving the required EPR of 2.24; however, this can be less than maximum thrust due to ram effect of the incoming air. Maximum thrust is obtained by holding brakes until static EPR is achieved or by promptly pushing power levers up during a rolling takeoff. At least two Airplane Flight Manuals recommend obtaining desired EPR before reaching 60 K.

Stall Margin

At normal rated thrust a turbine engine is operating at its design stall margin. With a specific power setting (EPR) selected, several situations can affect engine performance—for example, a sharp nose-up attitude, or severe turbulence as in the mishaps previously described (Fig. 8-3); a decrease in air density due to increased altitude; increasing inlet temperatures by applying inlet bleed air heat without a reduction in EPR; and especially a combination of these factors. At high angles of attack or in severe turbulence, inlet airflow may not enter the compressor section evenly and some blades may stall. Such airflow distortions can quickly lead to compressor stalls in a thunderstorm.

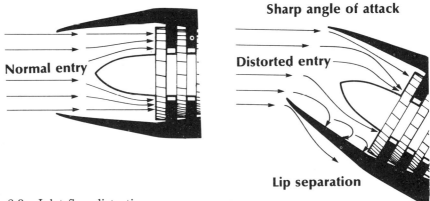

FIG. 8-3.   Inlet flow distortion.

Running up behind another jet (a good way to get foreign object damage) and the continued use of reverse thrust at too slow a speed will cause surging or stall as the compressor ingests the hot exhaust gases. Each of these situations reduces the inlet airflow (air density with heat), which reduces the compressor's ability to maintain its compression ratio. Finally, the hot air reduces compression ratio to the point that back pressure predominates. When this occurs the compressor stalls.

The continued modernization of various turbine engines has resulted in an increase in their compression ratios. To provide stall-free operation throughout the power range from idle to maximum thrust several innovations are used. The more common are variable inlet guide vanes (IGVs), variable stator blades, interstage compressor bleeds, computer operated surge bleed valves, and in some engines dual spool compressors.

The IGVs regulate inlet air to the compressor. At idle they are closed down to avoid problems of low engine speeds and high fuel flows; but they go to full open above approximately 70% RPM (Fig. 8-4). If they stick open during rapid deceleration, compressor stalls are a certainty. The fourth stage compressor bleed, found on the Pratt & Whitney JT12-6 and JT12-8 engines, acts similarly in the 79–81% range except that it is fully closed above 81% RPM and open below 79% RPM. The GE CF700 uses both IGVs and variable interstage bleed.

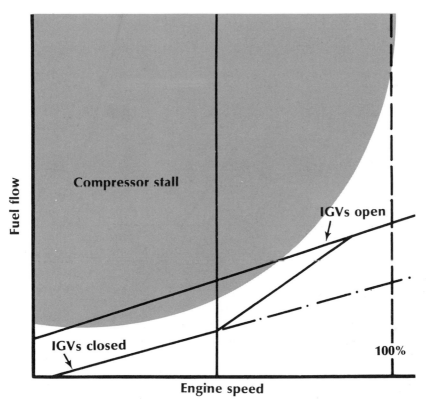

FIG. 8-4. Typical compressor operation curves.

The IGVs regulate the amount of incoming air; the compressor bleeds dump air overboard at selected points from the third, fourth, and fifth stages, preventing a buildup of high back pressures when the throttles are advanced rapidly to full power or reduced suddenly to idle. The Garrett TFE 731 uses an electronic computer to regulate a surge bleed valve system. If an imbalance develops between compressor RPM (or pressure) and amount of airflow, the bleed system opens to relieve the back pressure and vents it into the fan duct. Should electrical power fail the bleed valve fails to a partially open position.

Compressor Stall/Surge

As mentioned earlier, an engine operating at rated power is very close to its designed stall margin. The compressor is providing maximum discharge pressure, but the back pressure caused by the burning and restricted gases in the hot section is at peak value too. Therefore any disturbance (such as airflow distortion due to inlet ice buildup, compressor blade damage, severe turbulence, or even blade corrosion) lowers the stall line. Even a buildup in engineering tolerances in the chord or shape of compressor blades can result in sudden unexplained stall at high altitude.

Because compressor blades and airfoils are shaped similarly, a compressor stall can be compared to the stall of an airplane's wing. The aircraft wing stalls when its angle of attack becomes too great and the airflow separates from the upper surface so that it no longer produces enough lift to support the aircraft. A similar phenomenon occurs with a turbine engine compressor blade. At a constant RPM, when airflow directed to the compressor is diminished below a certain level (for example, in turbulence or an extreme nose-up attitude) one or more compressor blades will stall. The reduced inlet air velocity becomes too low for the compressor blades to create enough lift to continue a normal pressure increase. The airflow becomes unstable and the blades stall.

A stall that is limited to a few compressor blades in a relatively small area is no problem, since the remaining blades will assume the extra load. The situation may not be detectable by the pilot since airflow is only slightly reduced and no sudden increase in exhaust gas temperature (EGT) results. This is called a *cold stall* (Fig. 8-5). A compressor usually stalls asymmetrically; airflow in the stalled area is severely restricted, but airflow continues around that area.

Thunderstorms contain severe up- and downdrafts coupled with a high water/hail content that can result in severe airflow disturbances, as the incidents cited show. In an extreme case all the compressor blades stall and the airflow through the engine drops drastically. EPRs dip or fluctuate and EGTs overtemp quickly. In a complete stall combustor pressure can cause a complete airflow reversal with fire literally shooting out the nacelle inlet. With some engines the "report" from this action may sound like a cannon fired just outside the window. In others the engine may sound as if it is coughing, which it is. In either case it is guaranteed to get your attention. This situation is known as a *hot stall* and overheat damage or compressor/stator blade interference is the usual result. Severe internal damage is very likely.

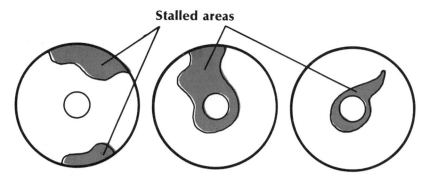

FIG. 8-5. Partial compressor stall (looking directly into the engine inlet).

Tests have shown that as the water content in the air increases an engine's stall margin decreases. At lower altitudes where air density is greatest the water content of the air can be quite high before surge or rollback occurs, but at high altitudes the weight of airflow into the compressor is relatively low.

The Reynolds number effect also reduces the compressor's stall margin. The Reynolds number is the relationship between air viscosity and its momentum, which depends on the aircraft's indicated airspeed. When this factor is coupled with reduced air density at altitude the amount of water required to exceed critical water/air ratios is reduced significantly. Therefore in thunderstorms between 30,000 ft and 40,000 ft, severe compressor stalls or a complete "drown out" is a distinct possibility.

When changing power from idle to maximum thrust, acceleration is normally smooth and follows the operating line in Fig. 8-4; but if the IGVs malfunction or the compressor bleed valves stick closed, a compressor stall results. During deceleration too, if the IGVs fail to close down as RPM decreases or if the compressor bleed ports fail to open, the engine compressor will stall. This problem is often caused by a faulty fuel control.

After landing on snow or ice and maintaining reverse thrust below the recommended 60–70 K stow point, the engines should be checked carefully, well back on the first and second stages for ice ingestion damage. That compressor stall could have been caused by exhaust gas ingestion, foreign object damage, or both. Don't wait until V_R during the next takeoff to find out.

Antiicing/Deicing

Whether flying a jet or turboprop the pilot should keep ohe eye on the outside air temperature (OAT) gage. Antiice heat should be on before encountering visible moisture, since deicing is the cause of ice shedding ingestion damage. It is easy to forget that engine inlet ice can form anytime visible moisture occurs in temperatures as warm as +5°C (40°)F. It is due to Venturi effect caused by the inlet's shape.

Some pilots believe that passenger comfort during descent is more important than the need for drag devices (speed brakes or spoilers). This is because of the buffet created. In reality their use is exceedingly important so that power can remain high enough to ensure adequate bleed air for engine inlet antiice heat. Every winter idle descents result in engine compressor or fan damage. Can you imagine executives so bothered by the noise of speed brakes or spoiler buffet that they're willing to pay $22,000–$44,000 for ice-shedding damage repair following a trip?

Sometimes at night or in weather, pilots not only forget inlet antiice heat but become preoccupied and forget to check visually for ice accretion. With a steady ice buildup the first clue may be the engine instruments—EGTs begin to increase while EPRs slowly decrease. If you are caught with your switches off and ice has already formed on nacelle inlets, the following procedure (recommended by GE for their CF700 engine) is good advice for any turbine. If your first move is to turn on inlet heat you are wrong. Instead:

1. Activate the continuous ignition system. In some instances it will be necessary to exceed the duty cycle limits; however, having ignition on may prevent a flameout when the ice sluffs off.

2. Ensure that engine RPM is above the minimum required for icing conditions, 75–85% RPM in most aircraft.

3. Activate dual engine nacelle antiice switches one at a time. With a single switch, as in the Sabre 40, 60, or 80, pull one engine antiice circuit breaker. (In the Sabres you'll prevent nacelle inlet lip heat but still get engine inlet heat at the guide vanes and bullet nose.)

4. If the engine stalls when the ice sluffs off, retard the throttle rapidly to idle. Then, if the compressor has quit surging, advance the throttle slowly to about 85%. GE reports that engines incurring compressor damage from ice ingestion will usually operate stall-free up to 85% RPM (it depends on the amount of damage incurred.) If a setting is reached as the power levers are advanced that causes resumption of compressor stalls, retard the power to whatever level provides stall-free operation.

5. Select full hot on cabin heat to increase cabin airflow. By using more compressor bleed air the stall margin is increased somewhat.

6. If the engine is stall-free at 85% RPM, a higher power setting can be used provided there is no sign of compressor stall such as audible report, engine rumble or vibration, RPM hang-up, or rapid EGT rise.

When the first engine has stabilized repeat the procedure on the second engine. Keep in mind that if your Flight Manual does provide a procedure for this problem you must use the FAA approved technique for your airplane.

Thunderstorms

Even the most conscientious pilot can inadvertently become involved with a thunderstorm or severe turbulence. The fact that engine inlet airflow distortion can (and does) cause double engine flameout should be ample motivation to avoid severe-looking cumulous buildups by the 20 mi recommended in the AIM and radar manuals. While a double flameout is relatively rare, it illustrates the extremes in airflow direction that can be encountered inside a cumulonimbus and the ultimate penalty of a massive compressor surge.

Most airplane flight manuals tell pilots that if they should enter a buildup the engine procedures are:

1. Change thrust only in case of extreme airspeed variations (especially important in heavy rain and hail).
2. Place continuous ignition on to help prevent flameout.
3. Engine inlet heat should be on and power maintained at a level sufficient to provide adequate bleed air. Ice always occurs in various forms in and around a thunderstorm.

If, as in the Southern DC9 case, it becomes necessary to descend while in heavy rain and turbulence, keep the power up—at least as high as minimum antiice requirements. A higher RPM withstands water ingestion better than an idle setting. Besides, an RPM rollback at idle in most aircraft results in loss of generators. If you must change power settings while in a thunderstorm or severe turbulence, make throttle movements very slowly and ascertain that RPM and EGT are stabilized before selecting a new throttle position. If, in heavy rain, the RPM has rolled back (decreased) do not advance the power because compressor stalls are inevitable. Just wait a moment until the rain diminishes and the RPM will recover.

Bird Strike

A bird strike can cause extensive compressor damage and lead to either flameout or compressor stalls. Since most bird strikes occur below 3000 ft, with the majority in the traffic pattern, the manufacturers recommend takeoff and landing with continuous ignition on. If a bird strike results in compressor stalls you are almost assured of damage. But, more important, power must be reduced immediately to a setting that will relieve the stall. If idle is reached and the stalls continue, the engine must be shut down. A restart can be attempted, but if the stall resumes the engine must be secured.

Slush

Slush damage occurs in a couple of ways. Using the Sabre 80 as an example, tests (unpublished) have shown that slush is most likely to cause compressor stalls between 70 K and 90 K. With continuous ignition on the stalls will clear and the engines continue running. If continuous ignition is not used the engines flame out. At these relatively low speeds the chine tires create a spray pattern from the nose wheels that sends the water or slush directly into the engines.

A second slush hazard occurs when you least expect it. It's a cold bright winter's day as you take the active runway; temperature 30°F (−1°C). The snow has been plowed but a residual coating has melted and formed puddles at intervals along the length of the runway. You begin takeoff roll and pass through the slush without obvious problems. But once airborne you discover some hefty ice formations around the nacelle inlets that were caused by departing with *inlet heat off.*

If, during takeoff from a wet or slush covered runway, a compressor stall occurs before V_1, an abort is recommended. You don't know whether the stall resulted from foreign object damage, slush ingestion, or a fuel control malfunction. Besides, you now have an unknown takeoff distance because of the power interruption and slush drag.

Your engine and the airplane are somewhat like the human body. Most of the time you notice more than adequate symptoms when something is wrong. When your engine coughs take immediate corrective action. Then before your next flight find out why. Because what you don't know or don't do *can* hurt you.

9

Departure and Deep Stall Phenomena

. . . HOW THEY OCCUR

SPIN TRAINING was eliminated from pilot licensing requirements around 1948. Future designs were to be stall/spinproof. Yet in 1980 several of the most popular single and twin engine aircraft will not only spin but are quite prone to flat spin, from which they will not recover. In the light twins a good part of the problem has been the lack of information concerning V_{mc} and how it is obtained. Although stall/spin mishaps are statistically a small part of the overall accident picture, during the 1970s from 28% to 48% of General Aviation fatalities were due to this cause.

The alarming fact is that one-third of the light twin accidents have been training flights. And stall/spin factors have been involved in several recent corporate jet landing accidents. Reading a textbook or magazine article can give you some of the important information needed to help you avoid a stall or a spin. But only through proficiency *and* knowledge of the slow speed and stall characteristics of your aircraft and spin training in an airplane approved for such maneuvers can you learn how to safely recover from an accidental loss of control.

Product liability lawsuits are encouraging better aircraft design, and NASA has uncovered some invaluable information regarding design features as they affect stall/spin characteristics. Using state-of-the-art aerodynamics the Gulfstream American Cougar, light twin trainer (now out of production), was built to be spinproof. Cessna's T303 Crusader is similarly spin resistant and foolproof at stall. The Robertson STOL modification for both twins and singles does a variety of good things such as lowering stall speeds and V_{mc} so that the modified aircraft becomes a safer and more docile vehicle. In the Seneca II, for example, V_{mc} with flaps extended is eliminated although a figure is published. And one model of a light trainer was given good positive spin recovery characteristics by installation of spoilers rather than ailerons. Before this conversion spin recovery was not guaranteed.

No rational person would deliberately spin a light twin or corporate jet because their spin characteristics are unknown and many are prone to flat spin. A number of stall/spin accidents have occurred in corporate and business aircraft, so some aerodynamic facts of life are worth reviewing. The terms *stall* and *spin* are used together not only because they are catalogued together by NTSB but because what a pilot does at the moment of stall results in either a recovery or loss of control. It's important to remember that a stall always precedes a spin.

V_{mc}

A misconception exists among a great many pilots that the yaw created by an engine failure should be corrected by using rudder alone (ball centered in the turn-and-slip indicator). This action is not only incorrect but dangerous, since by using this technique you can run out of rudder travel in any multiengine airplane at 10 to 20 K before the published V_{mc} (more in some jet and turboprop aircraft). The problem originates in a disparity between how the manufacturer obtains published V_{mc} and how engine failure training has been taught over the years.

During certification tests the manufacturer is allowed to establish V_{mc} "with an angle of bank of not more than five degrees." The speed thus established (ground and air) is always less than the "rudder only, ball centered" technique. In a staff study, Lester H. Berven (1976) described one typical light twin that has a published V_{mc} of 91 K. Yet in tests, using an aircraft equipped with an instrumented sideslip indicator and with the pilot applying the "wings level, constant heading, ball centered" engine-out technique, the aircraft went out of control at 115 K. In other words the aircraft can become uncontrollable at single engine best-rate-of-climb speed (V_{yse}; blue line). The staff engineers felt that a 5° bank into the operating engine would be "a normal reaction on the pilot's part to relieve some rudder pressure by banking." Yet until the 1980 revision, the only FAA training literature that even mentioned a 5° bank toward the operating engine gave it as a method of controlling the aircraft when an engine failed below V_{mc} (AC61-21 Flight Training Handbook). The problem is that some aircraft react so quickly there's not time to take corrective action.

In an unbanked twin, with the ball centered to correct for asymmetrical thrust, the aircraft is actually in a slight sideslip into the dead engine (Fig. 9-1). Installation of an inexpensive yaw string on the nose section shows this graphically. The large deflection required of the rudder results in increased drag that decreases rate of climb. This is easy to demonstrate with the Vertical Velocity Indicator (VVI) during engine-out training.

The Berven study emphasizes that "the single engine performance shown in the AFM (Airplane Flight Manual) is based on zero sideslip and is obtained by using an instrumented sideslip indicator." A yaw string serves the same

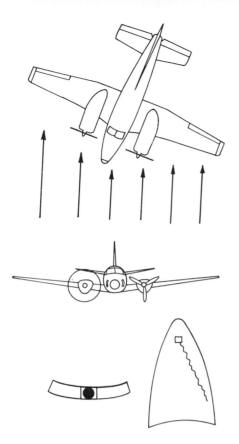

FIG. 9-1. With wings level and ball centered, the aircraft is in a moderate sideslip into the inoperative engine.

purpose and only shows zero sideslip with a bank into the good engine. For the majority of us, with no yaw string or sideslip indicator and a 5° bank applied, the ball in the turn-and-slip indicator becomes a bank indicator. At zero sideslip the ball will be approximately one-half ball out on the low wing (good engine) side. It is pulled there by gravity since the wing with the dead engine is up (see Fig. 9-2).

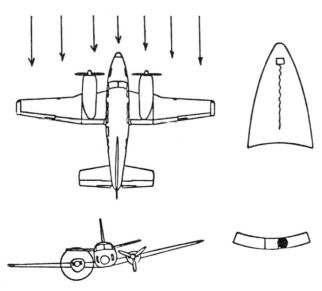

FIG. 9-2. Zero sideslip with 5° bank into the operating engine.

The following is a resumé of an interview conducted by the FAA with a flight instructor following a flat-spin mishap in a Beech Baron. The aircraft departed with a student and two flight instructors aboard and climbed to 4000 ft, where single engine procedures were practiced. Sometime later they landed and picked up another passenger and again climbed to approximately 4000 ft. Once at altitude the student was instructed to practice slow flight at 82 mi/hr—10 mi/hr below V_{mc}. At this low airspeed and with the aircraft in landing configuration (gear and full flaps extended), the instructor shut down the right engine with either the fuel shutoff valve or mixture (he couldn't remember which). At that point the student applied full power to the operating engine and the aircraft rolled right and immediately entered a flat spin.

The instructor promptly retarded the throttles and retracted the gear and flaps. The flight controls, he said, were dead and would not respond. First he tried normal spin recovery, which for the twins is simultaneous elevator control full forward, opposite rudder, and power to idle. Elevator is the primary recovery control (see Chap. 10). It was ineffective. For some reason he then increased power on the left engine, which increased the spin rate. Consequently he retarded the power and again extended the landing gear. The aircraft subsequently crashed on the roof of a supermarket, which undoubtedly saved their lives.

Several significant factors are involved in this accident. The additional weight of the two back seat passengers would not only tend to increase V_{mc} but also result in the center of gravity (CG) moving aft. With an aft CG an aircraft goes deeper into the stall, increasing the down elevator required to recover. In addition, an aft CG increases the tendency for a loss of control or for an accidental spin to go flat.

Some aircraft do not fully stall with full aft stick and a forward CG because of limited elevator "up" travel, a feature that helps prevent stall/spin problems. The Cessnas 152 and 172, the Piper Arrow, and the Sabreliners 40 and 60 are examples.

Remember that in a prop twin about 60–80% of the wing's lift is derived from the induced airflow of the propellers (see Fig. 9-3). This is why stall speed

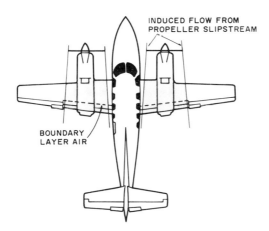

INDUCED FLOW FROM
PROPELLER SLIPSTREAM

BOUNDARY
LAYER AIR

FIG. 9-3. Influence of induced airflow from propellers on a wing's lift.

with power on is slower than with power off. When one engine suddenly becomes inoperative the induced airflow over the wing is lost. Therefore, at slow speeds just above power-on stall speed, a sudden engine failure causes the respective wing to stall; with a high power setting on the operating engine the pilot experiences both asymmetrical thrust *and lift*. The result is a sudden strong yaw and roll into the dead engine, which in some aircraft leads quickly to a flat-spin (Fig. 9-4).

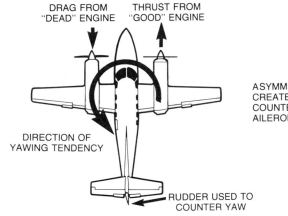

FIG. 9-4. Forces involved in obtaining published V_{mc}.

ASYMMETRICAL ENGINE POWER CREATES YAW WHICH MUST BE COUNTERED WITH RUDDER AND AILERONS

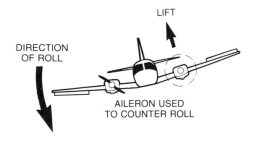

REDUCED AIRFLOW OVER THE WING DUE TO LOSS OF ENGINE PROP WASH RESULTS IN ASYMMETRICAL PRODUCTION OF LIFT. THIS MUST BE COUNTERED BY BANK INTO THE GOOD ENGINE.

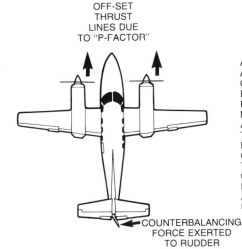

AT LOW AIRSPEED AND HIGH ANGLE OF ATTACK THE THRUST CENTERLINE SHIFTS RIGHT ON EACH ENGINE. THE DESCENDING PROPELLER BLADES PRODUCE MORE THRUST THAN THE ASCENDING BLADES (P-FACTOR). THEREFORE, LEFT ENGINE FAILURE RESULTS IN THE GREATEST YAWING MOMENT. THUS, THE LEFT ENGINE IS CONSIDERED THE CRITICAL ENGINE IN U.S. BUILT TWINS. AILERONS AND RUDDER MUST BE USED TO MAINTAIN CONTROL.

Extending gear and flaps will not aid recovery; it is best to retract them. The gear has no effect and incurs an airspeed limit during dive recovery, causing the pilot to rush the pullout with the very real possibility of causing a secondary stall. Flaps do not usually affect a spin; however on some specific designs the stalled wake of the wing and flaps can blank out the tail, resulting in either a locked-in deep stall (T tailed sweptwing aircraft) or a tumble, also called *departure* (loss of control). Corporate aircraft that have this problem are fitted with a stick shaker and stick pusher. The shaker activates 5–10% above stall; just before stall the pusher dumps the stick to prevent a loss of control.

Dynamic Effects on V_{mc}

The danger to the pilot in relying on the published V_{mc} for any given aircraft is that U.S. certification requirements provide a V_{mc} derived from a steady state flight condition. (FARs 25 and 23 both call for sudden engine-out but FAA policy is otherwise.) In other words V_{mc} is actually the slowest steady speed at which equilibrium can be achieved with 5° bank and full rudder deflection. Yet the significant effect of other dynamic forces should be considered.

An excellent study of this problem as it relates to crew training and training accidents by Air Line Pilot Association (ALPA) representatives Foxworth and Marthinsen (1971) is focused on dynamic effects relative to V_{mc}. The degradation in aircraft dynamics is thought to have led in several cases to sudden and violent deterioration of lateral and directional control, resulting in very rapid buildup of yaw and roll forces (inertia coupling) ending in disaster. The study gave several examples, one of which was the effect of crosswind on V_{mc}—a factor ignored in certification tests and which could be a causal factor in some recent corporate jet training accidents.

If an upwind engine fails during takeoff with a strong crosswind, the asymmetrical thrust coupled with the tendency to weathercock into the wind raises the minimum control speed, ground (V_{mcg}). How much is unknown, since FAA does not require this information. One airline published guidelines specifying "that for every 3 K of direct crosswind component the published V_{mcg} should be increased 2 K," which is similar to the findings of U.S. Air Force V_{mcg} tests of a multiengine jet.

The weight on the nose wheel at V_{mcg} is another important factor not addressed in FAA certification tests. Air Force tests have shown that down elevator during takeoff roll provides increased nose wheel side force (traction), which adds several knots to the effective V_{mcg}—"perhaps in excess of 20 K." If the runway is wet and slippery V_{mcg} will be higher than published, since certification is accomplished on a dry runway where nose wheel side force is good.

The British use a dynamic power application method to determine V_{mc}. Their system is endorsed by the International Civil Aviation Organization (ICAO) but is not used by the United States. To determine V_{mc} they "establish steady state unaccelerated flight at a low calibrated airspeed with zero yaw close to the predicted value of V_{mc}." Gear, flaps, and trim corresponding to the approach condition are added for realism. With the critical engine(s) inoperative and the throttle(s) on the remaining engine(s) at idle, power is suddenly advanced to maximum, obviously requiring optimum use of aileron and rudder. From the minimum control speed thus obtained a realistic V_{mc} is established. The ALPA study (Foxworth and Marthinsen 1971) states, "[using] this method would result in the most meaningful value of V_{mc} to pilots in line service who feel that V_{mc} must be determined under conditions which are typically duplicated during corrections to or abandonment of . . . engine(s)-out approaches. It is this value of V_{mc} which we do not know today . . . and it is the one most often abused."

V_{sse}

The use of V_{sse} (safe one engine inoperative speed), first emphasized by Beechcraft but used by other manufacturers as well, adds a safety factor to V_{mc} that significantly aids in controlling the dynamic factors just discussed. This is the speed "below which sudden power cuts of one engine will be prohibited."

To demonstrate minimum control speed in flight (V_{mca}) the Beechcraft communique (April 26, 1976) recommends that the engine be cut above V_{sse}. Airspeed would then be reduced until either V_{mca} or stall warning is obtained. To recover, power is not increased on the operating engine but reduced to idle with the nose lowered until V_{sse} is regained. The Beech communique also emphasizes the necessity for using a 5° bank into the operating engine.

Many of our light twins have a V_{mc} below stall speed. Therefore stall warning is the recovery signal.

The Deep Stall

The crash of Canadair Challenger prototype number 1 provides a valuable reminder to those few pilots of T tailed aircraft who ignore or disable safety devices such as the stick shaker and stick pusher. The Challenger was undergoing a series of stall tests with the artificial stall warning and stall barrier systems deactivated. Most T tailed corporate jets are subject to the deep stall phenomenon to some degree, but because they are good basic designs this characteristic is avoided by use of an artificial warning system. (The Diamond I and Citation III are exceptions—they do not have the deep stall problem.)

The so-called locked-in deep stall can be compared to a flat spin without yaw. The descent rate is very high. Aircraft angle of attack is well beyond the normal stall region, and because of this the turbulent wake of wings, flaps, and engine nacelles causes a complete loss in tail effectiveness. Instead of the aircraft pitching down as in a normal stall, it pitches up until stabilized at some very high angle of attack (Fig. 9-5).

Two factors that produce this nose-up pitch at stall are wing design (both sweep and section characteristics) and fuselage lift. In the first instance, when a sweptwing exceeds normal stall angle of attack, the tips may become totally stalled before the inboard sections even though the basic design allows for flow

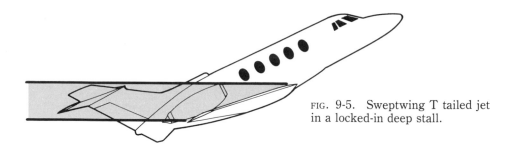

FIG. 9-5. Sweptwing T tailed jet in a locked-in deep stall.

separation (stall) to begin inboard first. The second factor, the forward protruding fuselage, continues to produce lift well after normal stall. Thus when the pilot causes the aircraft to exceed stall angle of attack, this fuselage lift contributes to the nose-up pitch (Fig. 9-6).

Once stabilized, the deep stall may not be apparent to the crew by looking through the windshield. However, the angle of attack indicator will show excessive angle and the elevator controls will buffet and feel dead. In addition the Instantaneous Vertical Velocity Indicator (IVVI; Vertical speed) will show a full-scale indication down—sometimes described as falling tail first. As with the flat spin, most aircraft will not recover. The point to remember is that the stall warning devices are there for a purpose—to prevent you from getting into trouble.

FIG. 9-6. Sweptwing jet experiencing tip stall with fuselage continuing to produce lift.

A note about T tailed straight wing aircraft, such as the King Air 200, the Beech Skipper, and the Piper Tomahawk. These aircraft have excellent stall characteristics. In addition the two trainers are excellent vehicles for spin training, since the rudder is always free of the stall wake of the horizontal stabilizer.

The Falcons 10, 20, and 50 and the Jet Star have their horizontal stabilizers mounted approximately midway up the vertical tail. The Jet Star does have the deep stall characteristic—no doubt the results of the expansive engine nacelle installation and the wing and flap wake. However the Falcon family is free of deep stall, with the nose breaking down cleanly at full stall. Heavy elevator buffet gives plenty of prestall warning.

Initial wind tunnel studies of the trijet Falcon 50 showed that with an aft CG a deep stall was possible. Because they wanted an aerodynamic solution rather than an artificial system, the horizontal stabilizers were redesigned with (anhedral) droop. Extensive flight tests at both forward and aft CG limits subsequently proved this to be the proper solution; the deep stall was never encountered.

A note about turboprops. Two basic types of engines are in use. The fixed shaft type is used in the Garrett TPE 331; the turbine wheel drives the compressor and reduction gear, which in turn drives the propeller. The second type is a reverse flow, free turbine engine found in the Pratt and Whitney PT6A. Here the three stage axial and single stage centrifugal compressors are driven by a single stage reaction turbine. A separate single stage turbine drives the propeller through a two stage reduction gear.

These factors are important when practicing approaches to stalls or when attempting a short field landing at a slow approach speed. At the first indication of stall (horn, light, shaker, or buffet) in the direct drive TPE 331, the pilot simply crams the power levers forward to maximum power and the engines provide instant thrust. With the PT6A engines more care is required. During any approach to landing the pilot should use drag to reduce approach speed while maintaining torque at 400 lb minimum. When firmly committed to land the pilot reduces torque, the prop pitch goes flat, and the landing is made. But if wind shear is encountered and the stall warning horn sounds, the torque must be increased slowly and carefully until above 400 lb—otherwise asymmetrical acceleration results and the aircraft quickly departs (goes out of control). I once rolled inverted because of this phenomenon in a King Air A90 when practicing approach to stalls with power at idle. At least one recent King Air C90 landing accident was due to asymmetrical engine spool-up.

Since we hope that no one would intentionally approach a stall or suddenly shut down an engine when close to V_{mc} with passengers on board, this chapter has been aimed at the training situation where a disproportionate number of stall/spin accidents occur. The point of emphasis is, "Don't make your initial or recurrency training so tough or hazardous that you can't pass your next flight physical."

10

The Accidental Spin

... AVOIDANCE AND RECOVERY

The Light Twin. The surviving pilot was not a professional but held a recently obtained commercial license. At the time of the accident he had approximately 270 hr and was in training for additional ratings under the GI Bill. The mishap occurred on his second flight in a multiengine airplane, a Beech Baron. The flight school's chief instructor occupied the right seat. Unfortunately another flight instructor sat in back to observe the training.

On their first flight some two weeks previously they had performed various orientation maneuvers such as shallow and steep turns, slow flight, stalls, and a V_{mc} demonstration. During this flight they concentrated solely on stalls: no single engine work, just power-on and power-off stalls with both engines running. The student said he noticed it took more nose-down pitch to recover than in the Cessna 172 he had been flying. He even encountered a couple of secondary stalls during recovery practice. "The whole plane felt like a heavier machine," he told investigators.

When the mishap occurred the student pilot could not recall a specific stall or configuration that led directly to the spin. "I just remember we were doing stalls and then I remember, 'Here we are in a spin.' It was a flat-spin to the left ... the nose was very slightly below the horizon ... maybe 5°. Rotation was not as fast as ... in a [Cessna] 150 [normal upright spin] ... it was turning slower." The recovery attempt appeared correct for their light twin—elevator control full forward and opposite rudder. The instructor extended the landing gear "which didn't seem to have any great effect." Recovery controls were held (as best as the student could remember) until impact. The student commented that full nose-down elevator had no affect on the pitch attitude. "The only difference ... from the beginning of the spin and the last thing I remember is [*sic*] slightly slower rotation." He could not remember what was done with the throttles.

The Corporate Jet. This accident involved an Air Force T-39A Sabreliner. It was on a maintenance test flight. The test card called for a full stall "to check aileron and slat rigging." The T-39 does not have a stick shaker. The pilot told ATC he was beginning the stall at 16,000 ft. No other transmissions were received. The wreckage pattern showed that the aircraft crashed in a spin.

The Four Place Single. This fatal mishap involved a Grumman American AA-5A. This type aircraft has been unusually prominent in stall/spin accident history. The limitations section of the Owner's Manual states, "Spins are prohibited. In case of an inadvertent spin, recovery is effected by reducing throttle to idle, neutralizing ailerons, applying full rudder opposite to spin rotation, and applying full down elevator simultaneously with rudder application. The controls should be applied briskly and held until rotation stops."

The pilot owner and his son-in-law departed late in the afternoon on a local pleasure flight. Witnesses, who included the owner's wife and daughter, saw the aircraft stall and spin through about three turns. It then recovered and began a second spin of about four or five turns. A second recovery was attempted at low altitude. Unfortunately it was unsuccessful and the aircraft crashed in a flat-spin. The owner's son told investigators that his father "always did spins because he enjoyed doing them."

All three mishaps had the stall spin phenomenon in common, but several factors merit careful consideration. In the Baron accident there is no FAA mandated training requirement for commercial, multiengine, or ATP applicants to practice full stalls. In fact, the multiengine student is "disqualified if a full stall occurs" or excessive altitude is lost. Recovery from an imminent stall begins at the first indication of stall, such as stall warning horn or stick shaker, onset of buffet, or decay in control effectiveness. The stall warning horn activates 5–10 K above stall and the onset of elevator buffet is 10–15 K before stall. And, while not a factor in this accident, neither imminent nor full stalls are required with one engine feathered.

The T-39A mishap is hard to understand because neither the T-39 nor Sabre 40 will fully stall with only the crew aboard—an inherent forward CG and limited elevator up deflection prevent a full stall. With elevators full up in a 1 G stall the aircraft simply buffets and pitches slightly. Ailerons are still effective so long as both of the aerodynamically operated leading edge slats extend. But if one slat sticks closed, the stall speed of that wing increases. Then if a full stall is attempted the unbalanced lift causes the aircraft to roll sharply into the wing with the retracted slat. The aileron too becomes stalled. So during the stall test with a hung slat, for example the right wing, the resulting sharp roll to the right would likely be countered by rolling the control wheel left. This deflects the right aileron down, resulting in a strong adverse yaw to the right (see Fig. 10-1). In aircraft with the weight primarily along the fuselage, the

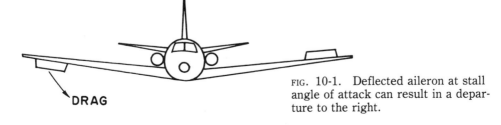

DRAG

FIG. 10-1. Deflected aileron at stall angle of attack can result in a departure to the right.

adverse yaw from a downward deflected aileron can be more powerful than rudder. An attempt to roll left would therefore *increase* the right rolloff into the stalled wing.

The manufacturer of the AA-5A has gone to great lengths to inform pilots that the aircraft is not certified for spins. Most light airplanes with only the two forward seats occupied (forward CG) recover quickly with opposite rudder and control wheel neutral. Some aircraft are exceptions; because of certain design features they are vulnerable to accidental flat-spins. The modern single engine, four place airplanes studied that have a recommended "stick full forward" recovery invariably have a history of flat-spins. Full forward stick is a desperate attempt to unload angle of attack.

Types of Spins

Three basic types of spins are: (1) upright, (2) inverted, and (3) flat. The *upright spin* is most often encountered and is usually recoverable except for designs in which the tail is blanked by the wake of wings and flaps. One four place trainer winds up so tight that the rudder lacks the power to stop its rotational inertia. This airplane now has limited elevator-up travel to prevent a full stall (unless it is loaded to an aft CG with passengers, for example).

The *inverted spin* is relatively rare because inverted flight is only practiced by aerobatic pilots. An accidental introduction can result from falling out of the top side of a loop, slow roll, or zero airspeed demonstration. An inverted spin is especially confusing since roll rate is opposite yaw. In nonaerobatic flight an inverted spin can occur from an upright attitude. Following an accidental *departure* (momentary loss of control such as a snap over the top), if the pilot suddenly remembers "elevator controls full forward" and in a panic crams the controls forward and holds, he will not only expose the structure to negative gravity overstress but very likely tuck under and enter an inverted spin.

The *flat-spin* is unique in that it consists entirely of yaw. It is especially hazardous, since for all but a few specialized aerobatic airplanes it is unrecoverable. In either the singles or twins that are known to spin flat, two pilot-induced factors are involved. Following an accidental departure, the pilot (1) continues to hold back pressure on the controls (to bring the nose up) and (2) increases (or fails to reduce) engine power. An aft CG contributes to a flat-spin also because the aircraft stalls more completely with the back seats and baggage compartment loaded. Unfortunately the record shows that flat-spin mishaps too often involve slow speed or V_{mc} demonstrations with the back seat occupied.

Spin Phases

Although some manufacturers use different terminology, NASA breaks a spin into three basic phases: (1) incipient, (2) steady state, and (3) recovery. Each phase has important characteristics that the pilot must understand (Fig. 10-2).

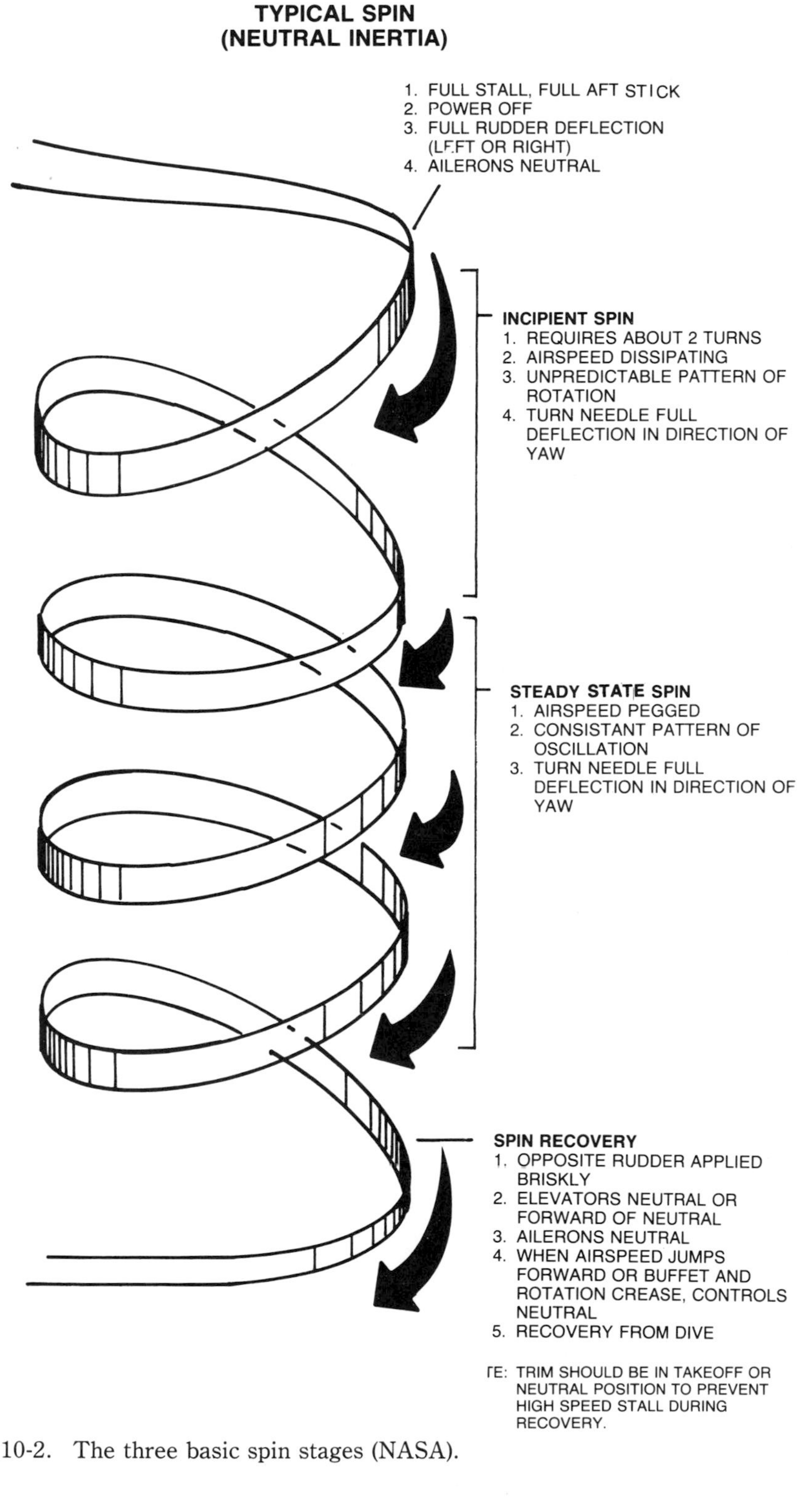

TYPICAL SPIN
(NEUTRAL INERTIA)

1. FULL STALL, FULL AFT STICK
2. POWER OFF
3. FULL RUDDER DEFLECTION
   (LEFT OR RIGHT)
4. AILERONS NEUTRAL

INCIPIENT SPIN
1. REQUIRES ABOUT 2 TURNS
2. AIRSPEED DISSIPATING
3. UNPREDICTABLE PATTERN OF
   ROTATION
4. TURN NEEDLE FULL
   DEFLECTION IN DIRECTION OF
   YAW

STEADY STATE SPIN
1. AIRSPEED PEGGED
2. CONSISTANT PATTERN OF
   OSCILLATION
3. TURN NEEDLE FULL
   DEFLECTION IN DIRECTION OF
   YAW

SPIN RECOVERY
1. OPPOSITE RUDDER APPLIED
   BRISKLY
2. ELEVATORS NEUTRAL OR
   FORWARD OF NEUTRAL
3. AILERONS NEUTRAL
4. WHEN AIRSPEED JUMPS
   FORWARD OR BUFFET AND
   ROTATION CREASE, CONTROLS
   NEUTRAL
5. RECOVERY FROM DIVE

NOTE: TRIM SHOULD BE IN TAKEOFF OR
   NEUTRAL POSITION TO PREVENT
   HIGH SPEED STALL DURING
   RECOVERY.

FIG. 10-2. The three basic spin stages (NASA).

The *incipient* phase for most airplanes is relatively long—two complete turns are normally required following a departure at near stall speed. If you banked and yanked at a higher speed (say 120 K) and thus have more energy (airspeed) at departure, it will take longer to go through the incipient phase and reach steady state. I've been told unofficially that a twin that flat spins may go flat *faster* when departure occurs with extra airspeed, e.g., from a high-speed stall.

In aerobatics a snap roll is a high-energy incipient spin. The incipient phase is characterized by an unpredictable pattern of oscillations that becomes more predictable as energy dissipates toward the steady state phase. The indicated airspeed can be seen to diminish with each oscillation. *Almost every aircraft flying will recover from an incipient upright or inverted spin or departure if the pilot will simply neutralize the controls.* If the elevators are not trimmed past landing approach speed (a good procedure in any airplane in slow flight), recovery is simply power to idle, feet on the floor, and hands on your thighs. Some heavier airplanes may continue rotation for another turn or so; in fact the oscillations may even accelerate just prior to spin recovery. Unfortunately it is the non–spin trained pilot who is most likely to panic and use a variety of control inputs and thus cause the spin to reach steady state.

The *steady state* phase is reached when (1) the indicated airspeed stabilizes and (2) the pattern of oscillation becomes consistent or predictable. At this point aerodynamic and inertial forces become balanced. In most good designs, even here, neutral controls will result in spin recovery, although it will take longer. To minimize altitude loss the pilot must now apply the manufacturer's recommended spin recovery controls.

The *recovery* phase begins the moment recovery controls are applied and continues until level flight is regained. In this phase antispin aerodynamic control inputs are used to destabilize the balance between the aerodynamic and inertia forces.

Two important factors are involved in this phase. (1) The pilot must be able to recognize the moment that recovery begins and release the controls. Recovery has occurred the instant airspeed jumps and starts increasing rapidly. The heavy tail buffeting also ceases. Rotation (roll) may not stop; in most light airplanes it does stop. In heavier types the stall may break but the aircraft continues in a diving spiral, which is corrected conventionally. (2) Rate-of-pull on the elevator controls during dive recovery is important. The nervous untrained pilot will rush pullout and at best encounter a high-speed stall or frequently the aircraft will snap back into another spin. This is why elevator trim during slow flight must not be full nose up.

Spin Recovery

Remember that there is no such thing as a standard spin recovery because aircraft designs are too variable. Following WW II, NASA conducted tests that showed a correlation between an aircraft's inertia moments and the control inputs required to effect spin recovery. Testing was required to verify their formula and it has been used ever since. For mathematicians the formula is $(IX - IY)/(Mb^2)$ where IX is roll inertia, IY is pitch inertia, M is mass (weight), and b is wing span (see Fig. 10-3).

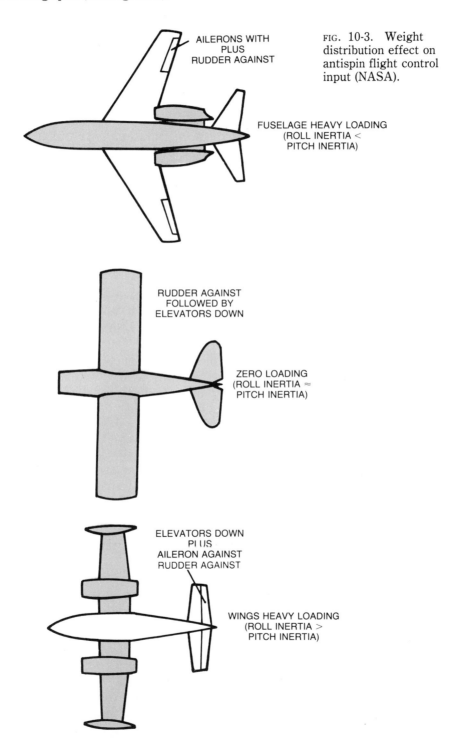

AILERONS WITH
PLUS
RUDDER AGAINST

FIG. 10-3. Weight distribution effect on antispin flight control input (NASA).

FUSELAGE HEAVY LOADING
(ROLL INERTIA <
PITCH INERTIA)

RUDDER AGAINST
FOLLOWED BY
ELEVATORS DOWN

ZERO LOADING
(ROLL INERTIA ≈
PITCH INERTIA)

ELEVATORS DOWN
PLUS
AILERON AGAINST
RUDDER AGAINST

WINGS HEAVY LOADING
(ROLL INERTIA >
PITCH INERTIA)

If the formula produces a zero or neutral answer (± 50) the aircraft is even-ly balanced. This includes all the light two and four place trainers and most aerobatic types. Spin recovery then is the so-called modified NASA recovery:

1. rudder against the spin (applied briskly) followed by
2. elevators neutral or slightly forward of neutral

Delay in applying down elevator (usually about half a turn) allows the rudder to begin taking effect. Apply forward stick too soon and the wake from the horizontal stabilizers can mask the rudder and reduce its effectiveness.

If the formula produces a negative answer, showing that the aircraft is fuselage loaded, aileron can become the primary recovery control. The Falcon 20 and DC9 are two examples. While opposite rudder is always required, the stalled wake of the horizontal stabilizer and engine nacelles often reduces rud-der power; therefore adverse yaw from a downward deflected aileron can be more powerful than rudder. In a spin to the left recovery controls would be

1. opposite (right) rudder
2. control wheel full left (which places the right aileron down)
3. elevators neutral or slightly aft of neutral

Holding elevators slightly aft of neutral helps keep the roll rate slow. Going for-ward of neutral causes spin rotation rate to accelerate. In this type of aircraft a panic application of full forward stick (elevators down) can result in a quick transition to an inverted spin.

Spin recovery for the fuselage loaded Sabreliner does not include use of ailerons because they are not fully stalled with the slats extended; therefore rolling the ailerons with the spin would likely increase the rotation rate. Con-versely, if a slat should stick closed the corresponding aileron would likely be stalled. With the right slat stuck closed the aircraft would roll right as stall speed approached. An effort by the pilot to stop the right rolloff by placing the control wheel full left would deflect the right aileron and result in a strong adverse yaw to the right. This action would therefore be the control input for a spin to the right.

Finally, if the inertia formula produces a positive answer the aircraft is wing loaded, or inertia moments about the wings predominate over inertia moments about the fuselage. This of course includes most of the light twins with wing mounted engines and wing and wing tip fuel tanks. In this case elevator is the primary recovery control. Recovery consists of

1. control wheel full forward (elevators down)
2. opposite rudder

Aileron against the spin can be used in some aircraft; however wing designs vary and most twin manufacturers recommend ailerons neutral during all spin recoveries.

This tells the pilot that if, for some far-out reason, a Falcon or Sabreliner or other corporate jet should encounter a spin, the procedure recommended for recovery is exactly opposite to that required for recovery in a Baron, King Air, Cessna 310, or Cessna 340. Even the differences in technique between the Sabre and the Falcon recovery could be significant.

Numerous exceptions to the $IX - IY$ formula rule exist. For example, a Cessna 337 is fuselage loaded, but the recovery procedure is control wheel full forward—likely the result of an aft CG tendency and the dynamic effect of the idling rear propeller. Some of the light four- and six-place singles are exceptions too. With a forward CG they spin and recover with opposite rudder and elevators neutral. But with all passenger seats loaded the CG moves aft; even though the aircraft may now be fuselage loaded, full down elevator is required to break the stall.

Landing Stall

Various models of the Learjet have been involved in three recent landing accidents and one takeoff accident where the stall/spin factor was involved. In each landing accident qualified witnesses saw the aircraft approach touchdown. In the Lear 23 crash at Richmond, Virginia "[the wings] started rocking, the nose came up, and the aircraft rolled right." At Anchorage and Detroit two Lear 25s were reported to "suddenly roll rapidly from side to side . . . and crash into the runway on a wing tip." In the fourth accident (also involving a Lear 25), which occurred during takeoff, the pilot may have had elevator trim set for landing rather than takeoff. The aircraft was seen to lift off abruptly and begin to roll from side to side. The aircraft struck the ground "slightly tail first with an increasing rate of descent."

Ice on the leading edges that increased stall speed may have been present on two aircraft. Strong, gusty surface winds that put the aircraft suddenly at stall speed in the flare may also have contributed. However, in the Richmond accident it was a clear calm night. Both pilots were low in jet experience and their final approach was reported as high with a long float before the crash. A sudden power reduction to idle in the flare could have left them close to shaker and stall speed.

Subsequent NTSB sponsored tests of Century III and Mark II modified Lears show that both types had satisfactory near-stall (imminent stall) characteristics. Wing aerodynamic rolloff of the Century III did not occur before the stick pusher activated. However little or no prestall airframe buffet was present; therefore a stick pusher that activates prior to stall is mandatory. The Mark II wing provides strong prestall buffet. Rolling tendencies generally started around 2 K above stick pusher speed; however, rolloff could be controlled within ±20° during entry and recovery.

With only small amounts of ice on the leading edges, the Century III wing experienced consistent aerodynamic rolloff prior to shaker activation. In landing configuration rolloff began around 10 to 12 K above pusher speed. With an 8° flap setting rolloff occurred 15 to 17 K above pusher speed. The study concluded that even small amounts of ice "on the wing leading edge . . . can negate

the entire stall warning system [shaker/pusher] of the Century III Learjet."
The obvious message to pilots is to use the wing antiice system as required by
the Airplane Flight Manual. The Mark II wing has the same antiice system as
the Century III. It therefore has the same susceptibility to ice on the outer wing
sections at minimum power settings. The Mark II wing with the simulated
leading edge ice showed an increase of only 2–3 K in stall speed. In addition
aerodynamic prestall buffet was "pronounced. . . . Rolloff started slightly
above pusher speed."

Further tests were conducted without ice shapes, using both the Century
III and Mark II wings. Go-arounds were made with the Century III wing from a
variety of conditions at airspeeds above stick shaker with no problems.
However, simulated go-arounds were made from a wing low, dragged wing tip
condition at speeds in stick shaker range. "Rapid pitch and rolling inputs were
made before adding power. The downgoing wing was observed to stall and
resulted in roll angles nearing vertical." At least 100 ft of altitude was invariably lost before control could be recovered. The Mark II wing, at the same
shaker speeds and wing low, go-around conditions, had similar results. "A tar-
dy application of takeoff power . . . would permit the downgoing wing to stall.
Roll reversal was not achieved before descent through the simulated runway
plane."

To pilots this means: Do not get below V_{ref} (landing reference speed,
$1.3V_{so}$) and into the shaker range on landing. The aircraft must be flown to the
runway. Remember V_{ref} is 1.3 velocity of stall with touchdown occurring
around 1.2 velocity of stall. (New landing approach speeds have been published
for the Lear.) Conversely, shaker airspeed is 1.1 velocity of stall or slightly less.
Wind shear from gusty surface winds is the most likely cause of sudden
airspeed loss and stick shaker activation. To avoid an inadvertent departure
remember that the Lear Pilots' Manual and those of other corporate jet
manufacturers recommend adding one-half the wind gust factor to V_{ref}. It
should be carried to touchdown. Landing roll must then be increased ap-
propriately.

Wing spoilers in place of full ailerons for roll control eliminate a great deal
of the problem in all categories of airplanes. For example, a right control wheel
input against a left departure provides a strong antispin drag factor on the
upgoing wing. Improved designs, such as the twin engine, nonspinnable
Gulfstream American Cougar and Cessna T303 Crusader are giant steps in the
right direction.

Remember that every airplane, like the personality of every pilot, is the
product of compromise. Therefore you must pay attention to the Airplane
Flight Manual and fly within the authorized performance envelope.

PART FOUR

The Landing Phase

11

Landing Considerations

... MORE THAN MEETS THE EYE

O N C E you break out on final with the runway in sight, the hard work is over; all that remains is the landing. A pro can do that without thinking, right? Apparently some pilots subscribe to that idea, yet 42% of General Aviation accidents occur during approach and landing. According to Robert Breiling, former vice president of Associated Aviation Underwriters, most landing mishaps in business aviation are overshoots; i.e., the aircraft skidded off the end. In most instances the runway was "too short" for existing conditions (it was wet, slushy, or snow covered). Also, he reports that reverse thrust malfunction is a factor in many of these accidents. Yet the FAA approved landing distance charts for every aircraft are based on crossing the runway threshold at 50 ft with an airspeed of $1.3V_{so}$ (V_{so} = stalling speed), and stopping with brakes only.

This information indicates that pilots are ignoring several important landing considerations. The number of landing errors would probably decline if the figure derived from the Normal Landing Distance chart was used as a base measurement that can grow larger—sometimes much, much larger—when certain adverse conditions exist. And they often do (Fig. 11-1).

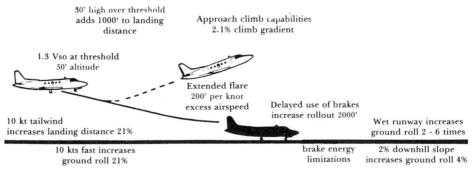

50' high over threshold
adds 1000' to landing
distance

Approach climb capabilities
2.1% climb gradient

1.3 Vso at threshold
50' altitude

Extended flare
200' per knot
excess airspeed

Delayed use of brakes
increase rollout 2000'

10 kt tailwind
increases landing distance 21%

Wet runway increases
ground roll 2 - 6 times

10 kts fast increases
ground roll 21%

brake energy
limitations

2% downhill slope
increases ground roll 4%

FIG. 11-1. Hazards in landing.

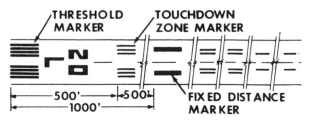

FIG. 11-2. Precision instrument runway marking (*Airman's Information Manual*).

Note that we have been referring to *landing distance*. As with takeoff distance, an obstruction is included in the calculation. A landing ground roll chart is not required. Under the current landing concept you are expected to cross the threshold at 50 ft and then touch down at 800–1000 ft. A precision instrument runway has the touchdown zone marked with three stripes and large rectangular boxes (Fig. 11-2).

Wind Direction

The aircraft checklist often provides landing distance figures for only a no wind situation. The Sabre 60 includes a 20 K head wind condition as well (see Fig. 11-3). With a tail wind on final (a condition becoming more common due to noise abatement considerations), the pilot must use the Aircraft Flight Manual charts to get accurate landing distance figures. Without a copilot this duty is often neglected.

If the flight manual is inaccessible, the pilot about to land can use this aerodynamic rule: A head wind that equals 10% of landing speed decreases landing distance by 19%. For a 90 K touchdown, a 9 K head wind will reduce an 1800 ft landing distance by 342 ft. On the other hand, a tail wind blowing at

ANTI-SKID OPERATIVE – ZERO RUNWAY SLOPE – DRY SURFACE
DISTANCES–FEET (FROM 50 FT OBSTACLE)
STANDARD ISA CONDITIONS

LANDING GROSS WEIGHT FINAL APPROACH SPEED	PRESSURE ALTITUDE – FEET							HEAD–WIND
	SEA LEVEL	1000	2000	3000	4000	5000	6000	KNOTS
17,500 LB	2930	3030	3150	3235	3340	3480	3675	0
126 KIAS	2560	2655	2750	2825	2910	3030	3225	20
16,000 LB	2720	2800	2900	3000	3090	3210	3395	0
120 KIAS	2380	2450	2540	2630	2710	2820	2975	20
14,000 LB	2425	2510	2590	2675	2750	2860	3020	0
112 KIAS	2125	2205	2270	2350	2410	2510	2660	20
13,000 LB	2260	2340	2400	2500	2575	2680	2835	0
108 KIAS	2000	2075	2115	2200	2250	2350	2500	20

FIG. 11-3. Landing Runway Requirements chart (*Rockwell International*).

10% of the landing speed will increase landing distance by 21%. Thus an otherwise modest landing of 1800 ft would be lengthened to 2178 ft. Keep in mind that this presumes maximum braking effort on a dry runway with new tires.

Runway Slope

Runway slope is a relatively minor consideration that has caused numerous erroneous landing decisions. The aerodynamic rule in this case is that a 1% runway slope will increase or decrease takeoff or landing distance by 2–4%, depending on the specific aircraft. Most aircraft fall into the 2% category. The NOS (National Ocean Survey) airfield diagrams (runway slope is not listed in the Jepps) show that the greatest slope found on airfields worldwide is 2%.

Therefore, when landing uphill at Aspen, which has roughly a 2% slope, the corporate pilot can at best expect normal landing distance to decrease 4%. For example, a corporate jet or turboprop landing on a 70°F (21°C) day (7800 ft field elevation) may have a no wind, no slope landing distance of 3600 ft; the 2% upslope will decrease landing distance by about 4% or 144 ft.

With a 10 K tail wind the landing will consume almost 4200 ft, a 726 ft increase (3600 − 144 + 726 = 4182). From these figures it is obvious that, given a choice, it is usually better to land downhill into a head wind than uphill with a tail wind .

Excess Airspeed

One of the prime causes of overshoot landings is excess airspeed on final. Many pilots, especially those flying cabin twin and turboprops, approach the runway at a speed considerably above the 1.3V$_{so}$ figure from which the landing distance charts are computed (Fig. 11-4). They mistakenly hold blue line (in FAR 23

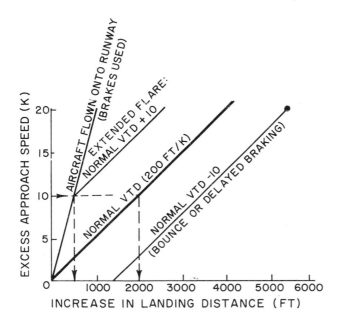

FIG. 11-4. Effect of excess approach speed on landing distance (may vary by type).

twins), which is marked on the airspeed indicator, until crossing the runway threshold even though this blue line figure is V_{yse} for the airplane at maximum gross weight. (This practice is a holdover from basic multiengine training in unsophisticated light twins.) To illustrate, the King Air 200 at maximum weight, 12,500 lb, has a V_{yse} of 121 K. Yet at a modest gross weight of 11,000 lb, V_{ref} ($1.3V_{so}$) is 99 K. Meanwhile V_{yse} has diminished to 117 K.

A frequently used landing technique with the turboprops is to extend full flaps at the last minute, dive toward the threshold, pull the power to idle, and rely on the flat pitch of the propellers to act as speed brakes. This practice indicates faulty training and is contrary to the FAA recommended procedure described previously.

During a fast approach the propellers help dissipate excess airspeed, but the aircraft invariably floats to at least the 1000 ft mark. Meanwhile, the pilot is exposed to the possibility of a premature touchdown short of the runway or, with a sudden go-around, runs the risk of slow asymmetrical engine spool-up to full power.

If the aircraft is flown onto the runway with excess airspeed, a three point landing is the usual result. In an extreme case, a nose wheel first touchdown can result, followed by porpoising. Discounting reversers, you can figure that a 10% excess touchdown speed will increase landing distance 20%. Since most municipal runways in the United States are 4000 ft or better, a 300–400 ft increase in ground roll appears negligible.

In the larger faster FAR 25 certified jets the situation is even more critical. Landing distance increases approximately 200 ft/K of excess airspeed bled off in an extended flare. Ten knots of excess airspeed at the threshold can extend the landing flare 2000 ft. Bouncing after initial touchdown or a delay in actuating reversers, brakes, spoilers, retracting flaps, or activating brakes has the same effect on landing distance as trying to dissipate excess airspeed in the flare (see Fig. 11-4).

Many pilots jeopardize their landing roll by attempting a smooth touchdown. By flying the aircraft onto the runway, an excess of 10 K airspeed can be dissipated in 200–600 ft (depending on runway surface conditions) using spoilers, reversers, and brakes. In other words it is three to ten times more effective to bleed off excess landing speed with the brakes, aerodynamic drag, and reversers than to attempt an extended landing flare (float).

Glide Path Effect

A turbine powered airplane (turboprop or jet) is required to fly the ILS (instrument landing system) or VASI (visual approach slope indicator) glide slope, even though on VFR, "until a lower altitude is necessary for a safe landing" (FAR 91.87d[2] [3]). A sound rationale supports that requirement. A normal 3° glide slope should result in a 500–600 ft/min descent rate, placing the aircraft over the threshold at the desired 50 ft altitude for a touchdown about 800–1000 ft long. If a flatter approach is used (let's say about 2°) or if the runway has around 1% of downhill slope in the touchdown area, the distance to touchdown can increase 1500 ft.

Crossing the threshold high also contributes to runway overshoot. For example, if you cross the fence 25 ft high your dry runway landing distance increases by 500 ft. Or if you cross 50 ft high (100 ft total) landing distance increases by 1000 ft. As a rule of thumb your landing distance is increased 200 ft for every 10 ft of excess height (Fig. 11-5).

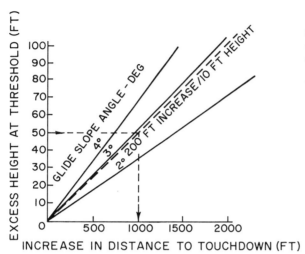

FIG. 11-5. Effect of excess threshold height on landing distance.

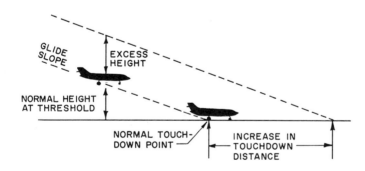

Wet Runway Factor

Joint NASA and U.S. Air Force tests show that as a general rule if the runway is wet the landing ground roll will be doubled; that is, the wet-to-dry stopping ratio is 2:1. For some reason FAA has not publicized these findings to FAR 91 operators. Worse yet, both Accelerate/Stop and Landing Distance charts are applicable only to dry runways. On many major airports where traffic is heavy, rubber buildup in the touchdown area may result in a 6:1 wet-to-dry ratio. Think of rubber buildup as wet ice. The effect is the same.

Note that a grooved runway or porous friction course (PFC), listed on the Jepp Approach plate or NOS Airport Facility Directory, provides an approximate 1:1 wet-to-dry ratio. Lateral grooves give excellent traction and the inevitable rubber deposits can be easily cleaned. A PFC, while equally as good in eliminating slipperiness, does accumulate rubber in the landing touchdown zone. In time it loses its drainage capability and becomes slick.

A crosswind combined with a wet runway can prove especially hazardous. If the high-speed touchdown area is exceptionally slick because of moisture and the buildup of rubber deposits, a crosswind will cause the aircraft to drift toward the downwind edge (Fig. 11-6). For aircraft that weathercock into the wind, the use of reverse thrust, a fixed beta prop setting, or a drag chute will not only increase the weathercocking tendency but also accelerate the sideways drift. Therefore the pilot must land toward the upwind side of the runway crown so that more runway width is available to absorb the drift. The pilot should beware of puddles on either side of a well-crowned runway. If one main gear is decelerating due to slush drag from the water, and the opposite gear is on a slick surface, directional control will be difficult.

Weathercocking and lateral drift can be checked with reversers if more

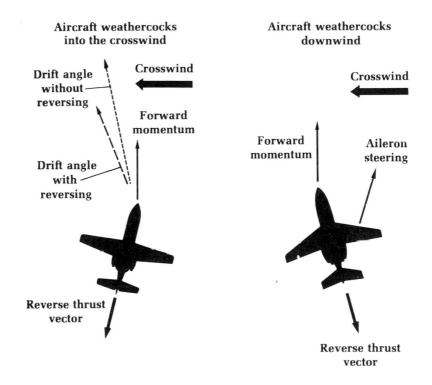

FIG. 11-6. Effects of a crosswind and a wet runway.

power is applied to the downwind reverser. For example, when the crosswind is from the right, apply more reverse power to the left engine than to the right and the aircraft will track straight down the runway. This technique is very effective in the King Air series.

Crosswinds affect the Sabre 40 and 60, BH125, DC9, and Hansa in an odd way. For various aerodynamic reasons these aircraft weathercock downwind in a crosswind (see Chap. 13).

Pressure Altitude and Temperature

Unless you frequent high elevation airports it may be difficult to realize how significantly the landing gross weight and the landing distance are affected by high pressure altitude and hot ambient temperatures. Transport category airplanes have maximum landing weights based on both structural and approach-climb considerations. At high elevation airports approach-climb is often more limiting.

Approach-climb is to landing what the second segment is to takeoff. In effect the aircraft must be light enough to miss an approach following engine failure and climb with approach flaps extended and gear retracted at a 2.1% gradient. Maximum thrust is used on the operating engine. Using the Sabre 60 as an example, the structural landing weight is limited to 17,500 lb at sea level. Yet on a 90°F (32°C) day at Colorado Springs, elevation 6200 ft, the allowable landing weight for the aircraft (pressurization on) with approach-climb limitations is 16,600 lb (Fig. 11-7). A heavier weight will allow no approach-climb (single engine go-around) capability.

The FAR 23 twins are not certified for single engine go-around. However the Single Engine Climb chart will indicate whether the intended landing weight is too great for the pressure altitude and temperature. If a single engine rate of climb capability remains, it is not too heavy. Keep in mind that single engine climb in these aircraft is accomplished with flaps and gear up and the prop feathered on the inoperative engine.

True Airspeed Factor

Landing distance increases with pressure altitude because true airspeed increases 2% for each 1000 ft increase in elevation. Thus for a King Air 200 at a gross weight of 11,000 lb on a calm 85°F (29°C) summer day, the landing distance over a 50 ft obstacle at a sea level airport is 2700 ft. Now fly into Cheyenne with an elevation of almost 6200 ft and the no wind landing distance increases to 3300 ft. This 22% increase is based solely on elevation. Now throw in a 10 K tail wind and the landing distance increases to 4300 ft. What if the runway is wet and ungrooved? Assuming the ground roll is 3300 ft on a dry runway, NASA's 2:1 wet-to-dry formula means ground roll in the rain (without

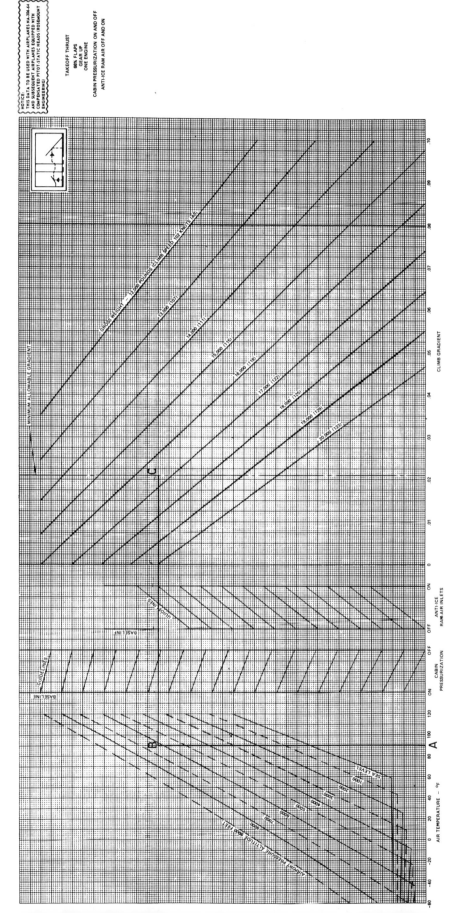

FIG. 11-7. Approach-Climb Configuration chart (*Rockwell International*).

reversers) will consume at least 6600 ft. If the aircraft touched down 10 K fast, add another 1320 ft (20%).

Plan each landing with the requirements of FAR 135 or 121 in mind. These two rules require that the landing distance must not be greater than 60% of the available (dry) runway. A 3300 ft landing distance would require a 5500 ft runway. If the runway surface is wet, an additional 15% must be added to the required runway length (a 3300 ft landing distance on a wet surface requires a minimum runway of 6325 ft). This may seem restrictive but an overshoot accident is even more so.

There's more to landing an airplane than making a smooth touchdown. Before every landing the pilot must carefully consider all the factors that can affect touchdown, or that smooth landing can get rough, very fast (Fig. 11-8).

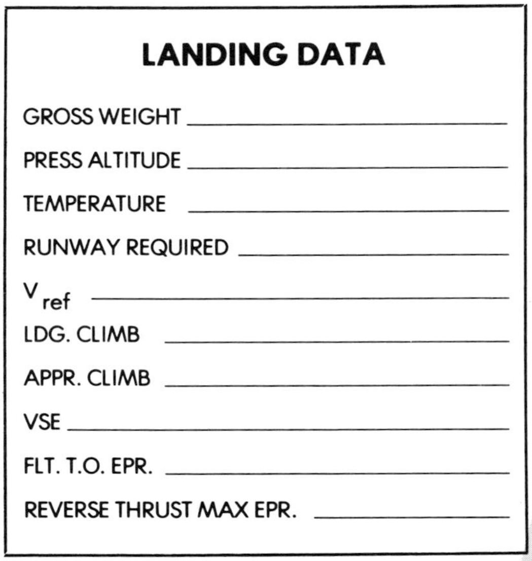

LANDING DATA

GROSS WEIGHT _____

PRESS ALTITUDE _____

TEMPERATURE _____

RUNWAY REQUIRED _____

V_{ref} _____

LDG. CLIMB _____

APPR. CLIMB _____

VSE _____

FLT. T.O. EPR. _____

REVERSE THRUST MAX EPR. _____

FIG. 11-8. Landing data charts.

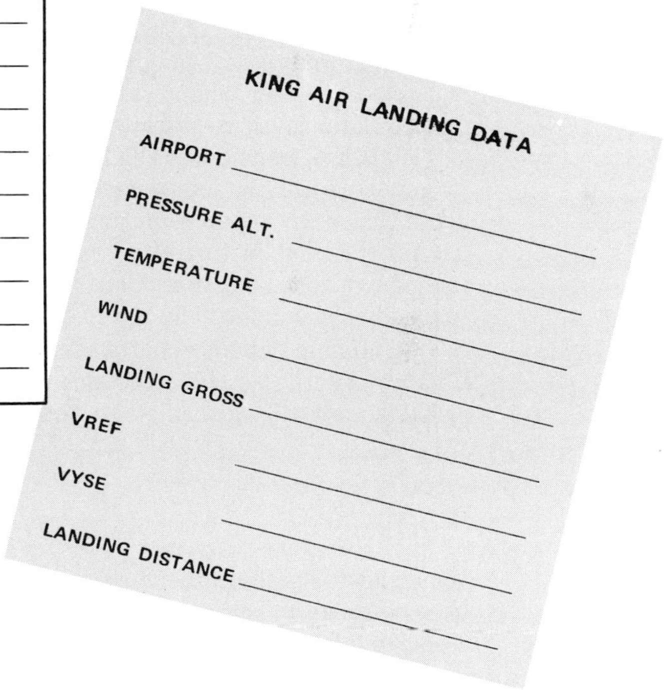

KING AIR LANDING DATA

AIRPORT _____

PRESSURE ALT. _____

TEMPERATURE _____

WIND _____

LANDING GROSS _____

VREF _____

VYSE _____

LANDING DISTANCE _____

12

Undershoot Landings

...A PERSISTENT CAUSE OF ACCIDENTS

L E T ' S L O O K at some of the factors that contribute to landing accidents. Touching down short of the runway, *undershoot,* is a major contributor and is the reason we are now taught to land 1000 ft down the runway. Other factors discussed in later chapters include crosswind landings on wet runways, underinflation of tires, and improper understanding of brakes and antiskid.

With the transition from small to large propeller planes to the larger, longer, and heavier jet transports, the undershoot accident rate became so acute that FAA began requiring that touchdowns be made 800–1000 ft long. To aid the pilot in this effort precision approach runways are painted with touchdown zone stripes and large white landing zone boxes to show where the touchdown should be. The ILS glide slope and VASI lead the pilot to this point.

All landing distance charts reflect this float from 50 ft over the threshold. This procedure has helped reduce landing mishaps, but several physical and visual factors still cause pilots to land short or undershoot.

Wind Shear

Wind shear is perhaps the most discussed factor. This phenomenon has always been with us in either of its two most common forms: (1) the gust front associated with a thunderstorm and (2) frontal movement.

Student pilots quickly learn that winds can be tricky in the vicinity of a thunderstorm. But for professional pilots the press of punctuality, mission accomplishment, or getting home often causes a tendency to press on into some hairy looking weather. We forget in our haste the AIM and radar manual warnings that severe storms should be avoided by 20 mi and all others by 10 mi. "We'll pick our way through with radar" is a common attitude. But the cells are often closer than the recommended 20 mi minimum. The problem is that weather radar paints only a cell's water shaft. The severe turbulence, hail, or (worse) tornadoes can be found a considerable distance from an intense cell.

Yet many pilots take the risk and continue an approach into varying rain and wind patterns. Most of the time they make it but a few pay the price.

For starters, the prudent pilot does not land within a thunderstorm's sphere of influence. According to Sowa (1974), here's why: the gust front or wind shear associated with a thunderstorm can extend for 10 to 15 mi along the sides and to the rear of a passing cell. Severe vertical drafts may be located near the gust front nose. A slow moving cell (slow meaning less than 20 K) usually has winds that blow out from the cell at 90° angles to the direction of movement (Fig. 12-1). A fast moving cell (like those found in Denver on a summer afternoon) has winds underneath and along the sides that blow in the direction of cell movement (Fig. 12-2).

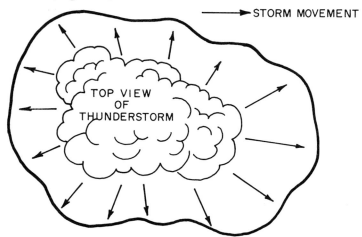

FIG. 12-1.   Surface winds resulting from thunderstorm downdrafts.

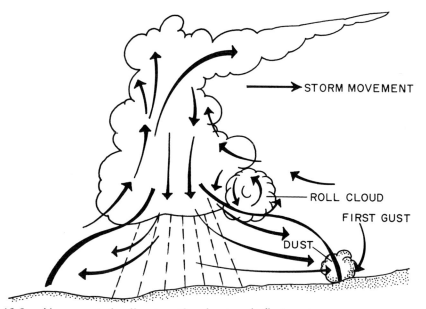

FIG. 12-2.   Air currents leading to a thunderstorm's first gust.

A classic example of this occurred one August at Denver's Stapleton Field. The prevailing wind pattern in the Colorado area was from the southeast. A fast moving midafternoon thunderstorm had just passed the field moving from approximately northwest (toward the southeast). The outside edge of the gust front remained over the field as evidenced by very gusty surface winds reported from 290°. There was bright sunshine to the west and south with a light sprinkle hitting the windscreen. The gust front wind pattern was characteristically blowing along the direction of cell movement.

I was flying copilot and we were landing a Sabre 80 on runway 26L. (As we were cleared to tower frequency on short final we overheard three airline crews discussing their hold for wind shear.) Because it was exceptionally rough the pilot was holding V_{ref} plus 20 K. Over the approach lights we experienced a classic head-to-tail wind shear. The gust front had passed and at the worst possible moment we encountered a 20 K tail wind. The pilot caught the sink rate, then touched down and brought in reversers. There was no problem, since we had extra energy (airspeed) to handle the sink rate and airspeed loss. The Stapleton runway is exceptionally long and would handle the sudden ground speed increase. Had we been holding V_{ref} at the threshold, an undershoot landing would have been inevitable. With the excess ground speed that results from a sudden tail wind shear, many general aviation runways may not be long enough, especially if they are wet and lack grooves or porous friction course overlay.

The same wind shear problem is present during frontal passage. With an approaching warm front, unpredictable winds can be present for up to 6 hr before frontal passage; then they settle down.

The exposure time is much shorter with cold front movement. As a general rule wind shear is most common just after a cold front passes. According to Sowa (1974), "To spot a possible problem two factors may provide the clue. First, if the cold front is moving at 30 K or more you should suspect wind shear. Another clue is the temperature spread across the front. If it is 10°F (5.5°C) or greater (cold to warm side) then wind shear is possible."

Visual Illusions

You no doubt remember from high school geometry that the arrangement of lines and curves can produce visual illusions. A pin-striped suit, for example, makes one appear more slim. So it is with the physical features of an airport and runway environment.

Five major characteristics of the landing runway can lead to the illusion of being high and cause a short landing or undershoot: (1) upsloping threshold terrain; (2) runway characteristics such as width or slope; (3) runway lighting; (4) runway contrast; and (5) visibility restrictions such as rain, snow, fog, haze, or even deicing alcohol on the windshield.

Sloping threshold terrain. From traffic pattern or FAF (final approach fix) altitude the approach zone terrain may appear level. Yet in mountainous or rolling hill country the threshold may have a definite upslope. Your final approach may even be over a valley. Without VASI or an ILS glide slope for assistance you perceive the approach height over the ground both under and in front of you. The upslope toward the runway causes you to feel higher than normal, encouraging a low flat dragged-in approach that exposes you to the possibility of a short landing. The airport at Clarksburg, West Virginia, carved out of a mountaintop, is an example of this.

On the other hand, if the terrain rises from the landing threshold the pilot will experience the illusion of being low on the approach path and will likely delay descent on final and tend to land long.

Runway characteristics. If you are accustomed to operating from wide, long metropolitan airports, such as Denver Stapleton, with 10,000–12,000 ft runways 150–200 ft wide, landing on a short, narrow runway can cause problems. Consider landing at Eagle, Colorado, with a 60 ft wide, 5000 ft long runway or Hilton Head, South Carolina, with a 75 ft wide, 3700 ft long runway. Long, narrow runways cause the illusion on final approach of being high. This illusion is intensified if visual clues are scarce because of a fresh snow cover that precludes accurate depth perception. If the threshold is surrounded by white beach sand and it is high noon on a bright clear day, your eyes can easily deceive you. Both situations can lead to a short landing.

Runway lighting. Bright lights appear closer than dim ones. On a dark night or low visibility approach with runway lights too bright the pilot will instinctively feel too high and lower the approach angle or duck under the normal glide slope. VASI or an ILS glide slope should be used here.

Over an unlighted approach zone with few lighted buildings to provide some depth perception, it is easy to misjudge and make the final approach too low. This difficulty is especially noticeable when the approach area is over a lake or bay, a dark green forest, or an expanse of desert. It is the well-known *black hole* effect.

Runway contrast. Lack of runway contrast can be especially conducive to short landings. A night landing on an unmarked VFR asphalt or macadam runway, especially if it's surrounded by trees, brush, or dark earth, can cause you to land short and hard. Without touchdown zone stripes the black runway and dark vegetation will absorb your landing light beam and distort your depth perception.

A fresh snow cover will have the same effect, especially in poor visibility, e.g., fog or snow showers. Without brush, trees, grass, fence posts, or runway markers you're as lacking in depth perception as a float plane pilot landing on a mirror calm lake.

Visibility restrictions. The various landing illusions seldom occur alone. Rain or snow on the windscreen, the alcohol deicer fluid used by some aircraft, dust, smoke, or fog—any of these can cause you to feel higher on the approach path than you actually are. Fog, dust, or dense haze at night also seem to absorb and diffuse the landing light beam and reinforce the tendency to drop low on the normal glide path. One source reports that refraction error resulting from rain on the windscreen can cause a pilot to fly as much as 200 ft low for each ½ mi from the runway. Cessna warns new twin pilots that the alcohol provided for windshield deicing can badly distort depth perception and cause a short landing. They suggest that the alcohol be off nearing MDA (minimum descent altitude).

Low Overcast and Low Visibility. A final visual trap involves an instrument approach into a very low overcast and marginal visibility. Most instrument pilots have an almost ingrained response to drop low on the glide slope once the runway is sighted, because the ILS glide slope tends to land you long. Apprehension over a wet runway creates a strong desire to touch down in the first 100 ft of runway. Consequently we have all tended to drop low in order to have more runway available. But several undershoot accidents that fall into this category have caused a renewed emphasis on staying with the glide slope until very near touchdown; for turboprops and jets it is required by FAR 91.87. Reversers or runway grooving will, we hope, take care of the wet runway factor.

The possibility exists that the pilot, once sighting the runway, visually aims for a touchdown area, and on short final when passing through a scud layer the runway begins to disappear. Then the pilot instinctively pushes over in an effort to keep the runway in sight. This results in an increased descent rate very low to the ground. With depth perception missing because of the low or nonexistent visibility, a hard landing or undershoot accident can result.

Landing Aids

Nine out of ten times you will encounter one or several of these visual illusions, combined perhaps with wind shear, yet despite these hazards you'll land without problems. But it's that tenth time, when you're tired or not feeling yourself, that the bright runway lights, the black hole effect in the approach zone, or rain on the windscreen causes you to land short.

To preclude this a pilot's ego ("I don't need crutches; my judgment is good enough") must be overcome. During instrument conditions fly the glide slope to near touchdown. When landing in rain—whether visual, day, or night—use the VASI to prevent dropping low due to water refraction error on the windscreen. At night on an asphalt runway without approach zone lights and without VASI, it is extremely easy to land short. Try to avoid this type of runway; remember the black hole effect.

Copilot call-outs of descent rate on short final can be exceedingly helpful. A rate of descent at touchdown greater than 600 ft/min usually means a hard landing or worse. After breaking out on ILS a sudden "descent rate 1000 ft/min" call-out indicates an inadvertent duck-under with obvious accident potential.

Remember: don't be too proud to use all the help that's available. It's better than trying to live down an accident—or heal up from one.

13

That Crosswind Trap

. . . AVOIDING LATERAL DRIFT

IN CROSSWIND ACCIDENTS one or more landing gear folds and the captain is tagged with a pilot error accident. Wet runway mishaps are not usually disastrous; they usually result in an embarrassed crew, an airplane off the side or end of the runway, and passengers deplaning through the mud.

Unfortunately, pilots tend to base a runway's suitability for landing primarily on prevailing visibility but wind direction and a wet, slushy, or icy surface are equally important. A crosswind and a wet, ungrooved runway can cause the airplane to drift toward the downwind edge. Thrust reversers, nose high aerodynamic braking, or an emergency drag chute can actually amplify the crosswind effect and increase the likelihood of an off-the-runway accident. (There are exceptions; ground roll characteristics and reversers combine in a few aircraft to minimize the crosswind drift factor, greatly expanding operational capabilities and safety.)

When landing on a wet runway in a strong crosswind, most aircraft tend to weathercock into the wind while the lubricated (wet) runway surface precludes effective traction. The effect is especially noticeable (and hazardous) in the high-speed portion of the landing roll when tire footprint pressures are light.

With low tire traction at touchdown and without benefit of thrust reversers, a crosswind causes an aircraft to drift slowly toward the runway's downwind edge (Fig. 13-1). This sideways push can be quite strong. NASA reports that "these [side] forces are proportional to the square of the crosswind velocity; thus a 10 K crosswind would quadruple the side force developed by a 5 K crosswind on an aircraft."

Crosswind Effect

Many of us tend to rely on thrust reversing to solve the slick runway problem, and with the wind parallel to the runway the reversers do the job. But a cross-

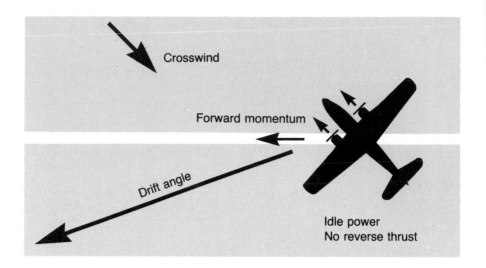

Landing at idle thrust on a wet runway can be dangerous—the slick surface precludes traction and aircraft weathercocks into wind. Resultant crosswind drift causes aircraft to move towards runway's downwind edge.

FIG. 13-1. Landing at idle thrust on wet runway.

wind combined with reverse thrust in an aircraft that weathercocks into the wind will intensify crosswind effect and accelerate the sideward drift (Fig. 13-2). Here's why.

Generally the crosswind's center of pressure on the fuselage is aft of the main gear—center of rotation—because more side area (fuselage and vertical

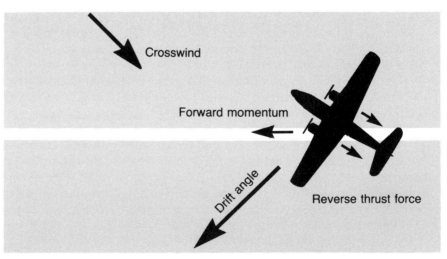

Reverse thrust can aggravate a bad situation—it actually acts parallel to the crosswind and increases rate of drift towards the downwind side of runway.

FIG. 13-2. Reverse thrust increases rate of drift toward downwind side of runway.

stabilizer) is exposed aft of the main gear. Consequently the aircraft wants to turn into the wind. After touchdown before reverse thrust is applied, the cross-wind begins pushing the aircraft toward the downwind edge of the runway (Fig. 13-1). Now bring the reversers in hard. The lateral drift increases because the thrust vector acts parallel to or with the crosswind (Fig. 13-2).

Then there's aerodynamic braking, a technique not recommended for any transport airplane on a marginal runway. With the nose held high to increase the frontal area there is some increase in induced drag; but tire footprint is very light, further reducing tire-runway interface (traction) and directional control. In addition, with tires lubricated by a wet or damp runway, that nose high attitude gives the crosswind more leverage and the weathercocking tendency increases. Again, downwind drift is accelerated.

Finally, in desperation, the drag chute is deployed. After all it is there for use on wet or icy runways. But with a crosswind the drag chute enlarges the frontal area, becoming literally a sail, which in effect moves the crosswind's center of pressure further aft and greatly increases the weathercocking tendency. Worse yet, it gives a mechanical advantage to the crosswind, which once again accelerates lateral drift (Fig. 13-3).

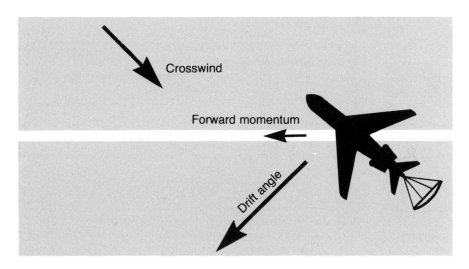

Deploying a deacceleration chute on landing moves the aircraft's crosswind center of pressure further aft than normal, increasing the weathercocking tendency and adding to crosswind drift.

FIG. 13-3.   Deceleration chute increases weathercocking tendency.

Exceptions to the Rule

The Sabreliners 40 and 60, the BH125, the DC 9, and the Hansa are exceptions. They weathercock into the wind on landing while the nose is still in the air. But lower the nose to the runway and each weathercocks downwind.

That BUF (Big Ugly Flugzeug) Hansa is unique in the drag chute department. The Hansa weathercocks downwind because it has more side area forward of the center of rotation. Its gear, like the Sabreliner, is narrow, thus allowing it to be tilted left or right with ailerons. Because it weathercocks downwind during landing roll and because aileron steering helps maintain directional control, a senior Hansa pilot reports no problem with crosswinds and wet runways. The BH125 too is an obvious case of more frontal area ahead of the gear.

The Sabreliners 40 and 60 are more subtle; with nose wheels on the runway the Sabre has a 13° angle of attack that effectively moves the center of rotation aft of the crosswind's center of pressure. Consequently, these aircraft also weathercock downwind. The nose low attitude and relatively narrow main landing gear allow the Sabre also to be tilted and steered with ailerons, thus providing positive directional control down to about 50 K. Because it weathercocks downwind, reverse thrust on the Sabre counters the crosswind induced drift (Fig. 13-4). Consequently it is easily controlled, even with nil braking action (although a landing with nil traction is not recommended).

FIG. 13-4. Reverse thrust on Sabre counters crosswind induced drift.

It is advisable to land any of the small corporate aircraft on the upwind side of the runway crown to take maximum advantage of runway width. A landing on the side of the runway and well off the crown can put one or both landing gear in the water drained from the runway crown. Also, after a snow the pilot must be wary of finger drifts caused by a crosswind. These fingerlike projections can become dense enough to cause sudden deceleration of the upwind gear and cause directional control problems.

The Sabreliners 70 and 80 are a bit different. First, their attitude on all three gear tends to be slightly nose up—a positive angle of attack due to CG and strut inflation. Aileron steering is not too effective unless the control wheel is placed well forward to compress the nose wheel strut. Then they can be steered with ailerons (tilted) much like their smaller predecessors. With a positive angle of attack on three gear and a larger fuselage area these enlarged Sabreliners do tend to weathercock into the wind; however their dual main wheels provide more positive traction and thus resist downwind drift. This situation is true also of the heavier double-wheeled Gulfstream II and Jet Star.

The Sabre still has the unique advantage of aileron steering in the high-speed touchdown area when nose wheels are incapable of traction on slippery surfaces.

I experienced a classic example of crosswind effect on Detroit City's 5000 ft runway 15 on a bleak December night in 1975. Weather was reported at minimums. A strong 40° right crosswind was blowing at 37 K. A twinkling red light atop a 200 ft smokestack just left of course helped remind us of minimums and encouraged careful wind drift corrections. The runway was blanketed by 2 in. of freshly fallen snow over a crust of refrozen slush. Traction was thoughtfully reported as "unknown." Our Sabre 40A touched down slightly on the upwind side at recommended speed. Immediate application of maximum reverse thrust and some aileron steering brought us to a near stop by midfield, centered between the runway lights.

A nonthrust reversing Lear behind us wisely diverted to Wayne County. A more tenacious Citation, also nonthrust reversing, did land but not without landing gear damage. We last saw him surrounded by red flashing lights.

Turboprop aircraft *can* be managed by using asymmetrical reverse thrust. When the power levers reach the reverse range after touchdown, slowly increase torque, leading with the downwind engine. As torque increases be sure that the nose remains straight down the runway. If it wants to turn downwind, decrease some torque on the downwind power lever. If it still wants to weathercock, increase torque on the downwind engine. Once you find the correct adjustment, bring both power levers back toward maximum reverse. An attempt to rush this procedure (as might occur on a short runway) can result in lateral oscillations. This technique works well in the King Air series. An aircraft, such as the Gulfstream I, in which the props have only a fixed flat pitch (beta) position for rollout will retain the strong weathercocking and lateral drift tendency.

The moral is that a wet or icy runway combined with a crosswind can mean "missed approach." If you are flying an aircraft that weathercocks into a crosswind, then even with reversers another runway or an alternate airport may be advisable. Above all do not accept an unfavorable runway based on noise abatement considerations. And if you are drag chute equipped, save it for another day. It is hard to "tack" an airplane but easy to "sail" off the side.

Those Neglected Tires

. . . THE IMPORTANCE OF TIRE PRESSURE

A TIRE PRESSURE check should be accomplished before the first flight each day. For some reason pilots neglect this important chore. At home base a mechanic may be asked to do it or maybe the company has a mechanic who accomplishes the entire preflight. On the road it's a different story. The pilot must see that it's done. Since many Fixed Base Operators (FBO) have only stick tire gages, the pilot should carry a precision tire gage. (A line mechanic of a major FBO once checked the tires of my King Air A90 with a stick gage and read a pressure of 50 psi, within the required 50–55 lb; my calibrated gage read 35 psi. The tire even looked low, although a visual check should not be the guiding criterion.) High pressure tires associated with heavier, high performance aircraft are more critical. With high-speed takeoffs and touchdowns, major accident potential is involved.

Even blow a tire on takeoff? I have, and at a heavy gross weight it's a handful until you are airborne. I was training a student for his Sabre 40 type rating. The tire blew at V_R so the logical procedure was to continue takeoff. The gear was left down, as most handbooks recommend, to allow air-cooling of the wheel and molten rubber. This practice also precludes the possibility of the mangled tire hanging in the wheel well. Some Airplane Flight Manuals do not address the subject. The basics are essentially the same from light twins to corporate and airline jets.

A blown tire during takeoff is frequently caused by foreign object damage from a rock or metal object. Underinflation is also a major cause. Previous damage from the heat of heavy braking, a hard landing, or perhaps mishandling during the tire-wheel buildup process are possibilities too.

In the Sabre 40 incident cited above the culprit was underinflation. The wheel rim, although recently dye checked, had developed a fatigue crack that allowed air pressure from the tubeless tire to seep out overnight. This wheel had been mounted the previous evening and both of us were reluctant to call out a mechanic for our 0800 Saturday morning training flight. And only the mechanic had access to the necessary equipment. The underinflated left main wheel was difficult to see with the aircraft sitting on the ramp. Both wheels were planted on a sagging section of old asphalt; the illusion was that of a tire sitting in a depression. After all, the tire was newly installed, so the pressure had to be right. Right?

Many pilots never give tire inflation a second thought. If they do think a tire looks low, it's usually too close to passenger boarding to round up the necessary people and equipment. And alas, at some locations, neither people nor the proper equipment are available. So preplanning is required.

The Tire Gage

Since a tire pressure check is a daily requirement, the cockpit crew must carry a calibrated tire gage. The FAA does not recommend the automotive stick type. (Try the accuracy check mentioned earlier of a stick gage and a recently calibrated pressure gage; if you really want to become a believer compare the readings given by two stick gages.)

There are two good reasons for the daily check. The first is that a 5% air loss in a 24 hr period is considered normal—a tire inflated to 180 lb on Monday morning is normal if on preflight Tuesday the pressure indicates 171 lb. It needs reinflating of course, but the tire manufacturer knows and expects some pressure loss every 24 hr. Despite this the flight crew is frequently on the road for a week without once checking tire pressures.

The second reason for carrying your own tire gage involves ambient temperature changes. Suppose you depart Miami on a 70°F (21°C) day in February and remain overnight at Teterboro where the early morning temperature is a cool 5°F (−15°C). This temperature drop means tire pressures will necessarily be less than required. In adjusting for changes in climate, Goodyear publishes a rule of thumb: "A 5°F (2.77°C) temperature change results in a 1% tire pressure change." So with a 65°F change from preflight at Miami to preflight at Teterboro, we'd expect a Sabreliner's 185 lb main wheel tire pressure to read about 161 lb. This 13% pressure loss is due solely to temperature change. Reinflation is mandatory. This effect also occurs in winter when an aircraft is preflighted in a warm 60–70°F (16–21°C) hangar and moved outside to cold-soak for several hours.

Tire stretch is frequently overlooked by mechanics. After a new nylon-reinforced tire is mounted on the wheel, a 24-hr stretch period is required before being installed on the aircraft. It can and usually does result in a 5–10% pressure loss in the first 24 hr.

A freshly mounted tube tire should be checked closely (Goodyear recommends a check before *every* takeoff) because in the mounting and inflation process air can be trapped between the tire and tube. This trapped air seeps out around the bead or valve stem and the result is a severely deflated tire.

Low Tire Pressure

Suppose you skip the tires during preflight and one or more are below the recommended standards. According to Goodyear, an aircraft tire operates at peak efficiency with a 32% flexing or deflection action. (An auto tire is designed for a 12–17% flex.) This design feature is a calculated compromise between shock absorption and optimum tread wear.

Heat and foreign object damage are a tire's two greatest enemies. Heat is generated during taxiing, takeoff, and landing by the designed flex of the tire carcass as it rotates over the pavement. The flexing action can be likened to the rapid bending back and forth of a piece of wire. With excessive bending it gets hot and breaks. When you taxi on an underinflated tire carcass, flexing is greater than normal and therefore heat builds up more rapidly than normal. High taxi speeds and long taxi distances increase heat buildup. For example, a 45% deflection can more than triple normal tire heat buildup; if it's also a hot summer day with an extended takeoff roll, you're playing a game called "you bet your carcass" (in fact every carcass on the airplane).

Another problem with low tire pressure, especially for nose wheel tires, is *burst deflation.* A hard turn, a sudden swerve, or a determined turn down the high-speed taxiway after landing, can literally roll the tubeless underinflated nose wheel tire off its rim. It happens every winter. Even if the tire doesn't deflate, a significant pressure loss can result.

Signs of Improper Inflation

We all know the telltale signs of routine operation with underinflated tires— worn tread on the tire's edges with the center ribs relatively intact. Overinflation is evidenced by excessive wear of the center ribs. Too much pressure robs you of some shock absorption but, more important, it diminishes the tire footprint and reduces available traction. It makes damp or wet runways even more hazardous.

Sound rationale exists for an operator to have an extra set of wheels in stock. Most dual wheels require careful matching in tread wear and pressure. With dual nose wheels, a worn tire (with less tread and therefore smaller circumference) or a tire with a lower pressure can cause a pull toward the edge of the runway. Because of the extra load imposed on the larger (new) tire, internal damage is possible. Nose gear shimmy and tire failure are also possibilities. With dual main wheels the circumference factor and inflation pressure are equally important. If the tires have unequal tread or pressure, the larger tire will carry more of the load; at high gross weights this can mean a blowout. Therefore a new and a worn tire should not be matched (see Fig. 14-1). Extreme wear on either edge of a worn tire may indicate a long period of underinflated use or the need for gear realignment. Even the outside diameters of new tires should be measured after the recommended stretch period, and pairs should be matched according to their measurements. You'll be surprised at how much tires vary.

FIG. 14-1. Uneven wear pattern shows need for gear realignment.

Perhaps the biggest argument for stocking spare wheels is the tire stretch period needed by new nylon-reinforced tires that in a 24 hr period can result in a 5–10% pressure drop. Also, some wheel rims require nondestructive inspection (NDI) following each tire removal. This check uncovers fatigue cracks in the wheel that can result in the previously mentioned insidious slow leak. A spare set of wheels precludes the temptation to skip this very important NDI check.

Preflight and Postflight

Several things must be checked during preflight and postflight. Tire pressures should be taken 2–3 hr after landing when the tire has cooled. Newly installed tires may require additional pressure if pressure was originally established on the bench. Under a maximum gross load most tires require a 4% pressure increase to compensate for reduced tire volume because of deflection due to aircraft weight.

Nitrogen is used to inflate most high pressure tires because it is less sensitive than air to temperature fluctuations and it is often difficult to find a compressed air source with pressures in the 185–214 psi range. Mixing air and nitrogen is allowed if no other choice is available.

To preclude excessive pressure loss due to a change from a warm to a cold

climate, destination temperatures can be checked and tires overinflated to account for the temperature change. Remember the rule, 1% for every 5°F
(2.77°C) change. An overnight stay on a cold ramp will necessitate reinflation
the next morning, so time must be allowed for it.

Tires should be checked for visible damage or excessive wear both on
preflight and postflight. For example, a rib with a cut greater than 50% across
or any ply damage calls for a tire change. Ever peel off a strip of tread on
takeoff?

Tread Wear

When the remaining tread reaches $\frac{1}{16}$ in., NASA tests show that the tire is for
practical purposes smooth. Therefore, traction loss on a wet or damp runway
or even a taxiway is probable. Beware the new and worn tire combination on
single wheel airplanes; the new tire provides more traction. With one main
wheel nearly slick and the other essentially new, directional control may
become a problem during heavy braking—especially with a wet runway–crosswind combination.

Check for tread separation. Any sign of groove cracking, rib undercutting,
rib bruising, or blistering requires removal. Chevron cutting caused by
touchdown on a grooved runway is usually minor and unless the cord is exposed it does not necessitate tire change.

For aircraft lacking a fully modulating antiskid system, flat spots can be
caused by inadvertent brake pressure at touchdown. Or you may find areas of
scalding due to reverted rubber skidding, a form of tire hydroplaning. This
phenomenon can occur at any speed and remain to under 5 K. Applying brakes
before wheel spin-up occurs is the most likely cause. These tires need not be
changed unless casing plies are exposed. However, if vibration or shimmy occurs the tire or tires must be changed.

On tube tires check for a tilted valve stem—the result of operating
underinflated. This condition in itself can result in a leak or deflation as the rim
cuts slowly through the valve stem.

A rejected takeoff with heavy braking, especially if the wheels or tires
become visibly hot after shutdown, requires a tire change. Bead or sidewall
damage most likely occurred. It would be false economy to take a chance.

Check for rocks; concrete spalling; or nuts, bolts, and screws on the ramp
and taxiways. Many airport managers are preoccupied with other details and
allow an unbelievable accumulation of debris on ramps, taxiways, and runways. (During a recent Sabreliner trip I found three airports in a condition un-
suitable for even a Cessna 150, much less the corporate jet we were flying.)
Prop, engine, and tire damage are the inevitable results.

Some maintenance work results in metal objects being scattered in and
around parking and refueling areas. A tight turn into parking with a bolt under
the tread, or taxiing out behind a turboprop slinging rocks, soft drink caps,
nuts, bolts, and screws can damage a sleek corporate jet.

In conducting corporate crew flight training I visit a variety of flight operations. Before each check ride I spot-check tire pressures. It invariably produces red faces. "We checked it last night before we left." But the tires were still warm following a trip and it's colder in the morning. Then, too, there's the allowable 5% seep, or a 10% nylon stretch, or an unfortunate slow leak. Yet with preplanning it takes less than 10 min to check and even reinflate every tire on the airplane. The professional checks. The carcass you save could be your own.

Getting Stopped

... OPTIMUM BRAKING TRACTION

WE'VE DISCUSSED various landing considerations and how each one affects landing distance. Today's professional pilots are seldom faced with a required maximum performance braking situation. Yet, not using a braking technique appropriate to the type of brakes installed may cause the pilot to end up ignominiously off the end of the runway.

Usually there's no reason to worry because under normal conditions we get all the braking we need; the long runways and normally reliable thrust reversers spoil us. Eventually the day arrives when we need all the traction we can get; getting it depends on touchdown speed, type of brakes and antiskid used, condition of tires, runway surface texture, and pilot technique (see Chap. 11).

Pilot technique using nonmodulated antiskid brakes is quite different from that required with a fully modulated system; and with manual brakes the pilot must be as cautious as a lovesick porcupine. For the airline pilot the ultimate is an automatic "select deceleration" system. This so-called brake-by-wire system allows the pilot to select the desired deceleration rate until manual takeover, when the system tunes out.

Brakes, as commonly understood, are designed to perform one simple function—stop the wheels from turning. With moderate brake pressure applied, wheel rotation is reduced and the frictional force generated between the tire and the runway causes the aircraft to decelerate and stop. This frictional force is described by the (braking) *coefficient of friction.* The maximum coefficient of friction is realized just shy of the point at which skidding occurs.

As the pilot applies brakes on a dry runway the friction rises until an 18–20% rolling skid is reached (see Fig. 15-1). At this juncture, even though the wheels are still rolling at 80% of their normal speed, maximum friction is achieved from the tire-runway interface. With a 20% rolling skid almost no skidding or slipping has actually occurred. Yet once this point of peak friction is passed, the tire locks in a total skid and braking friction diminishes rapidly.

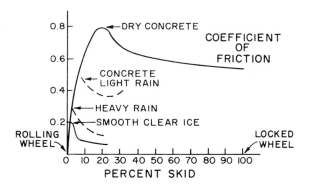

Fig. 15-1. Coefficient of friction as a function of percent skid.

When tires begin to skid the brakes fail to absorb any of the energy; instead the tires take the full load, usually with disastrous tread wear. What's more, skidding tires are uncontrollable. And once a tire wears through it blows out. Then you've got your hands full.

With high-speed, high pressure tires, two things happen in a skid on dry pavement. First, the rubber begins to scuff and tear off in small pieces that act as rollers underneath the tire. Heat generated by the skid begins melting the rubber. Then the molten rubber becomes a lubricant beneath the tire and destroys traction. During landing roll without antiskid, if a wheel inadvertently locks or if a skid develops on one side the aircraft will actually turn away from the skidding wheel rather than toward it. Further brake pressure is ineffective. To stop the skid and regain runway surface traction, the brakes must be *completely released* to allow the wheel to resume rolling. It all happens so fast a blown tire is the usual result.

History of Antiskid

In the mid-1950s the advent of higher performance turboprop and turbojet aircraft equipped with power brakes made it more difficult for the pilot to feel what was happening to the tires. Blown tire mishaps were common. Consequently an *antiskid* system was designed.

The original system compared rate of wheel-speed change with a fixed rate standard; when the standard was exceeded brake pressure was automatically released (see Fig. 15-2). This system simply prevented total wheel lockup. Its shortcoming was that no brake friction was generated during the antiskid release signal. The pilot applied strong brake pedal pressure; when a release signal was felt it was necessary to back off and release the pedal pressure and then reapply brakes. For best effectiveness the pilot had to search for the point just shy of the antiskid release. During panic braking, such as might be appropriate during a rejected takeoff, if the pilot failed to back off and search for the antiskid release point the result would be "strut walk" in some aircraft or heavy vibrations due to the on-and-off shuttle of the brake release valve. This increased stopping distances.

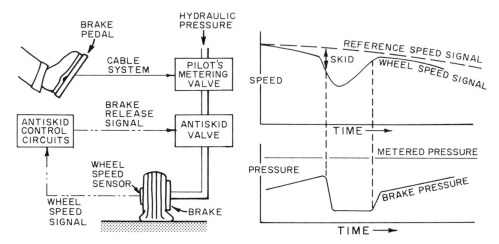

FIG. 15-2. Original antiskid system.

That first nonmodulating antiskid system was improved significantly and is currently and effectively in widespread use. New corporate jets are fitted with a *modulated* or *proportional* antiskid system. This unit, like its predecessors, is sensitive to rate of wheel-speed change. But the advent of a faster acting proportional servo valve allows controlled *automatic* reapplication of braking friction during periods of heavy use. The result is shorter accelerate-stop and landing rollout distances because the antiskid system, instead of the pilot, keeps hydraulic pressure just shy of the skid point.

Added to the modulated antiskid systems are such refinements as locked wheel protection on touchdown. Some aircraft have a wheel spin-up/spoiler actuation feature that kills lift and increases tire footprint pressure. The BH125 and HS125-700 have a lift dump system that extends the spoilers and increases flap extension angle and is exceptionally effective. Some airliners have nose wheel brake and antiskid systems.

Antiskid systems are designed to provide good stopping distances with minimum tire tread wear (or damage) on a *dry* runway. The FAR certification requirements do not require stopping capability demonstrations on wet runways because surface slickness varies so greatly at different airports. Instead, FAR 121.195 and FAR 135.385 provide that landing distance must not exceed 60% of the runway length. And for a wet surface, runway length must be 15% greater than the dry landing runway requirement (see Chap. 11).

Other Braking Aids

Since 1970, grooved instrument runways have been standard for federally funded construction. This all but eliminates the slickness factor caused by water or slush. NASA tests have shown that antiskid systems and tire tread design can only help make the best of what traction is available. The key to stopping is runway surface texture.

Tread design and degree of tread wear are factors, however. A tire having less than $\frac{1}{16}$ in. of tread performs as if bald. A new tire on a dry runway may provide a friction coefficient of 0.8 and a bald tire provides a coefficient of about 0.4; add moisture and take away thrust reversers and you can imagine what happens to ground roll.

Runway surface water can be dissipated to some extent by deep grooves in tire tread. The deeper the grooves and the more grooves the tire has (up to a point), the better it handles water and slush. Tire pressure is also a factor; you'll get more traction from a tire with 185 psi than from one of the same size with 215 psi because the higher pressure tire has a smaller footprint.

Hydroplaning

A pilot lucky enough to have a fully modulated antiskid system with locked wheel protection on touchdown cannot blow out a tire. This unique design protects tires from the dual hazards of heavy feet on the brakes during touchdown and from failure of the wheels to spin up after landing on a water film (*dynamic hydroplaning*). (See Fig. 15-3.)

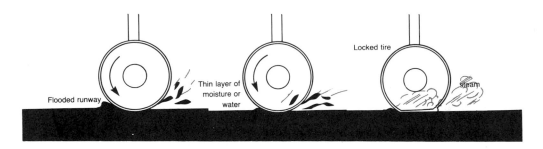

FIG. 15-3.   Three types of hydroplaning: (left) dynamic, (middle) viscous, and (right) reverted rubber.

NASA films made during hydroplaning tests show that when a high performance aircraft touches down on a wet runway, the wheels may fail to spin up because of hydroplaning. Without RPM (spin-up) at touchdown the non-modulating antiskid has no rate of wheel-speed change to compare with the fixed-rate standard. Since the locked wheel protection feature is absent, hydroplaning tires frozen by a pilot's brake application will encounter a dryer or less flooded section of runway and begin *viscous* or thin film skids and friction heat is generated.

The addition of heat changes the moisture to steam and a *reverted rubber* skid evolves (Fig. 15-4). Since this form of tire hydroplaning will continue down to a very slow speed (unless the wheels are allowed to resume rotating) the airplane is likely to slide off the side or end of the runway. Then, instead of the black skid marks you expect to find from skidding tires, the runway is marked

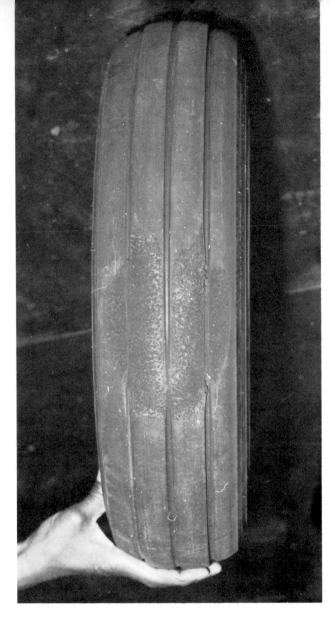

FIG. 15-4. New tire shows results of reverted rubber skid.

by characteristic white "steam clean" tracks. The tires may or may not blow out, depending on runway asperity and moisture level.

Smooth tires or tires with less than $1/16$ in. of tread remaining will hydroplane with only a slight water/slush accumulation. Even a heavy dew can precipitate viscous skidding.

To determine the likelihood of encountering hydroplaning (ungrooved or non-PFC), use the following general guidelines.

1. Light rain: viscous and reverted rubber hydroplaning likely at any speed (as low as 5 K). Dynamic hydroplaning is unlikely.

2. Moderate rain: all forms of hydroplaning possible. New tires are less susceptible than worn tires.

3. Heavy rain: all forms of hydroplaning.

Another situation that is similar to hydroplaning occurs on a hot day with uncured tar or smooth asphalt runways. A newly resurfaced or resealed runway can become dangerously slick as the summer sun softens it and bakes out its moisture. This kind of surface is also exceptionally slick when wet and should be outlawed, but General Aviation runways have no minimum standards. The Airline Pilots Association holds FAA's feet to the fire at major terminals so minimum fraction standards are maintained.

Deceleration Forces

To stop an airplane successfully the pilot must effectively use all the deceleration forces available. These include aerodynamic drag, reverse thrust (if available), and wheel brakes. The total braking force available is the sum of all three and is directly affected by touchdown speed, runway surface conditions (wet, dry, rubber coated), and pilot technique.

When either of the two antiskid systems is used, normal braking technique should be a light gentle pressure just after touchdown that is slowly increased to a heavier pressure as speed decreases. Intermittent braking, choppy and uncomfortable to passengers, is poor technique.

Maximum performance braking is quite different between aircraft with modulating and nonmodulating antiskid systems. With a fully modulating antiskid system the pilot must apply maximum brake pedal pressure; the antiskid controller then keeps the brakes just shy of the skid point. If the pilot attempts to modulate the brake pressure the system is defeated and landing roll is increased (see Fig. 15-5).

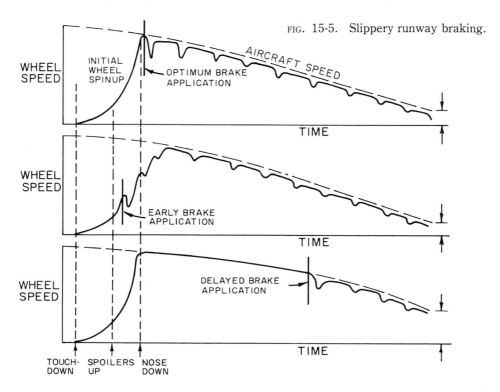

FIG. 15-5. Slippery runway braking.

With a nonmodulating system the pilot applies brake pressure to the point of an antiskid release signal and then backs off and attempts to keep the antiskid just shy of a release signal. If the pilot holds maximum pedal pressure (as in a panic stop), the subsequent release signals will extend the rollout.

On short or slippery runways pilots need all the help they can get. The amount of traction a tire-wheel can generate is proportional to its footprint (aircraft weight carried by each tire) on the runway. Consequently the pilot's first chore is to maximize aircraft weight on the tires immediately after nose wheel touchdown. The method used depends on the design of the aircraft.

Flaps up on touchdown. In the Sabreliners 40, 60, and 80 the flaps are retracted on touchdown, resulting in a sudden reduction in lift. If flaps remain extended only about one-third of the aircraft's weight is on the gear; wing lift supports the other two-thirds. On a dry runway this single action reduces landing ground roll by 13%.

The disadvantage of flap retraction is that aerodynamic drag is lost. In the Sabre some drag can be realized and the tire footprint pressure can be increased by pulling the control wheel smoothly full aft. However the nose wheel must be keep firmly on the runway by maintaining heavy brake pedal pressure. If the antiskid is cycling (slick runway) some control wheel pressure must be released or, with the nose wheels lightly tracking, directional control can become a problem. Keep in mind that this aft control wheel technique is for optimum braking. Some other aircraft recommend wheel full forward, e.g., the Westwind IA1124.

In the Sabreliners additional aerodynamic drag is obtained by extending the lower fuselage mounted speed brake during rollout; it shortens ground roll by 6%. Without thrust reversers, shutting down one engine and eliminating residual thrust will improve stopping distance by 4%. Securing both engines is even better although no figures are available. This technique is only for the Sabre since its hydraulic system is electrically driven rather than engine driven.

Upper wing spoilers. Many aircraft have upper wing spoilers just forward of the flaps that the pilot deploys on touchdown. These include the Raisbeck Sabre 60A, Lear series, Falcon series, Westwind, Diamond I, Citation series (upper and lower wing spoilers), and Boeing types. The BH125 uses a total lift dump system (described below). Extension of upper wing spoilers immediately after touchdown results in a sudden reduction in lift and an increase in aerodynamic drag. Deploying these spoilers (some call them air brakes) has the same lift reducing effect as retracting flaps. In the Falcon 20, for example, extending the air brakes during the high-speed portion of landing rollout results in 70% of the airplane's weight being placed on the wheels. The beauty of spoilers is that, in addition to increasing tire footprint, they provide up to 18% more aerodynamic drag—enough to be helpful on a slush- or ice-covered runway. But like all deceleration devices (including reversers) they must be activated promptly following nose wheel touchdown, since their effect is greatest in the high-speed portion of landing rollout.

Lift dump. The lift dump system used on the BH125 and HS125-700 series and involving both spoilers and flaps, is quite effective. These unique aircraft are fitted with double slotted flaps that permit landing at rather low airspeeds. At a typical touchdown gross weight of 15,000 lb, V_{ref} (landing approach speed) is 99 K and landing flaps are normally extended to 50°. After touchdown the pilot moves the airbrake lever to open, lifts it, and pulls back to the dump position. This action causes the upper wing air brakes (spoilers) to extend beyond the normal open position and simultaneously extends the flap angle from 50–75°. These two actions are like opening two large barn doors. The result is an immediate lift reduction of 62% while aerodynamic drag increases 47%. In many ways this design is superior to thrust reversers because reversers have a lag involved with deployment and engine spool-up. Then too, the reversers must be stowed at 60 K to avoid ingestion damage.

Thrust reversers and drag chutes. On a dry runway both reversers and drag chutes help relieve wear and tear on the brakes. Immediately after touchdown with spoilers extended, a Boeing study shows, aerodynamic drag and reverse thrust provide about 50% of the total deceleration force and brakes supply the rest. It varies with the type of reverser used. The clamshell or target type seems to be more effective than the more sophisticated Cascade system. The most effective system I've flown is the target type installation on the Citation II.

No figures are available for drag chutes. My experience has been that deploying the drag chute, especially with a reasonable head wind, will provide 90–100% of the deceleration force required. Many times following drag chute deployment I've found it necessary to add power to clear the runway. However most drag chutes have crosswind limitations of 15 K and the nose wheels must be firmly planted before deployment. The logistics of handling these chutes and their tendency to freeze at altitude after a wetting on the ramp make them useful only as an emergency measure.

Once the runway gets wet, slushy, or icy slick, reverse thrust and aerodynamic drag are about all you can rely on for decreasing your speed. In the high-speed touchdown area reversers provide at least 80% of the stopping force. At lower speeds the brakes should become more effective and provide about half the stopping force, but at times (when glaze ice covers the taxiways and ramp) it may be necessary to rely totally on reverse thrust.

Stopping Distance

As discussed in Chap. 11, the stopping distance in any airplane depends on touchdown speed, runway surface conditions, and how well the pilot uses the decelerative forces available. A touchdown speed 10 K too fast will increase landing ground roll from 10% to 21%. Excess touchdown speed is a major cause of overshoot accidents.

Wet runways are also involved in overshoot accidents. As a rule of thumb, a wet surface increases ground rollout from 60% to 100%. Key elements in getting stopped on a slick runway are (1) a prompt reduction in lift to increase tire footprint; (2) immediate lowering of the nose wheels to get them tracking; and (3) maximum use of brakes, reversers, and drag.

Delaying brake application until ground speed is less than tire hydroplaning speed, the so-called 100 K procedure, can increase ground roll as much as 25%. If excess touchdown speed is also present, rollout distance can become a problem. Keep in mind that some low pressure tires will hydroplane at speeds as low as 70 K. Viscous skidding, as mentioned earlier, can occur at any speed.

Brake-by-Wire

The ultimate in braking is achieved with the Hytrol Mark III select deceleration. It is a so-called brake-by-wire antiskid braking system that allows the pilot to select the best rate of aircraft deceleration based on passenger comfort and runway condition. For example, suppose a 4 ft/s² deceleration is selected for a normal metropolitan airport. The pilot lands and, without applying brake pressure, lowers the nose and actuates the thrust reversers. Wheel touchdown automatically actuates the brakes, which, working in coordination with the reversers, provide the selected deceleration rate. When reverse thrust is applied less brake pressure is provided. When the engines are spooled down the brake pressure increases. This procedure provides continuous deceleration at the preselected rate. The concept is to take maximum advantage of the brakes during the high-speed (touchdown) portion of landing roll. Manual braking is always instantly available to the pilot (see Fig. 15-6).

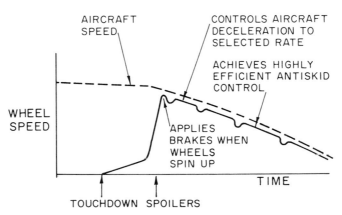

FIG. 15-6. Autobrakes on slippery runway.

For a rejected takeoff the same instant braking feature is available. With flaps in takeoff position maximum braking is applied automatically if the power is suddenly reduced to idle. A safety feature prevents inadvertent brake pressure during takeoff with full power applied. This system is presently available for the Boeing transports, the DC9, and the DC10; and can be fitted to most corporate aircraft.

Landing Distance

With gusty surface winds, some excess airspeed is required on final approach and landing. Manufacturers of all aircraft recommend carrying the gust factor across the threshold to touchdown and adding the excess rollout requirement to the landing distance. This is also the airline procedure. An increase in ground roll due to the added speed is infinitely better than a short hard landing. For example, if your final approach speed is 120 K with a computed landing distance of 4000 ft, an excess speed of 10 K increases total landing distance by only about 850 ft provided the aircraft is forced on. Should the excess speed be bled off in the air before touchdown, landing distance may be increased by 1500 ft.

Brake Heat

After heavy use the brakes will heat up. Generally temperatures do not peak until 5–15 min after use; therefore stop-and-go landings during training should be sandwiched between instrument approaches or the go-around should be accomplished with gear down to provide slipstream cooling. Otherwise the hot brakes may cause a fire or flat tire. The flat tire would result from melting of the fusible wheel plug or built-in tire thermal plugs that protect against wheel-tire explosions.

Air Force tests have shown that water can be used for wheel cooling if it is applied in 3–5 s squirts directly to the exposed portion of the brakes; then wait about 15 s and apply it again. The excessive heat has ruined the tires, of course, and they should be changed and discarded.

One final word of advice. Normally rudders are used with the pilot's heels on the floor. After touchdown when toe brakes are needed, the feet are shifted so that the rudder bar crosses the instep of each foot with the toes covering the brake pedal. Only from this position can maximum pedal pressure be achieved. Rudder pedal adjustment is very important, since full brake pedal pressure may not be possible when the rudder is fully deflected. Therefore when sitting in the chocks prior to engine start, check to see if your favorite pedal setting provides maximum brake pedal deflection with the rudder at full travel.

As you can see, a great deal of skill is involved in landing and stopping. Review your braking system and the manufacturer's recommended technique. Then, when the chips are down, your stopping power will be at hand.

BIBLIOGRAPHY

AOPA Safety Foundation. 1978. AOPA Handbook for Pilots. Aircraft Owners and Pilots Association, Bethesda, Md.

Air Training Command (USAF). Aerodynamics for Pilots. ATC Manual 51-3.

Bervin, Lester H. 1976. *Engine-out Characteristics of Multi-engine Aircraft.* Federal Aviation Administration, Washington, D.C.

Boeing Commercial Airplane Company. 1976. Landing on slippery runways. DC-44247. Seattle, Wash.

Bowman, James S. 1965. *Airplane Spinning* SP83. NASA, Langley Research Center, Hampton, Va.

Brantigan, John W. 1974. When being on oxygen is not good enough. *AOPA Pilot Magazine.*

Cobb, Jeve B., and Horne, Walter B. 1964. Performance on slippery runways in crosswinds. *Airline Pilot Magazine,* June 1964.

Davies, D. P. 1977. *Handling the Big Jets,* 3d ed. Daniel Greenaway and Sons, London.

Dreher, Robert C., and Horne, Walter B. 1966. *Ground-Run Tests with a Bogie Landing Gear in Water and Slush.* TN D-3515. NASA, Langley Research Center, Hampton, Va.

Federal Aviation Administration. 1978. Water, slush, and snow on the runway AC91-6A. Washington D.C.

Federal Aviation Administration. 1980. Instrument flying handbook AC61-27C. Oklahoma City, Okla.

Foxworth, T. G., and Marthinsen, H. F. 1971. The case against engine-out flight training. AIAA paper 71-793. American Institute of Aeronautics and Astronautics, New York.

General Electric. 1975. CF700 turbo fan engines SEI-189. Lynn, Mass.

Hirzel, E. A. 1972. *Antiskid and Modern Aircraft.* Society of Automotive Engineers, New York.

Horne, Walter B. 1965. Recent research on ways to improve traction on water, slush, and ice. NASA, Langley Research Center, Hampton, Va. Paper presented at AIAA Aircraft Design and Technology meeting, 15–19 Nov. 1965.

Hurt, H. H. Jr. 1965. *Aerodynamics for Naval Aviators.* U.S. Navy. NAVAIR 00-80T-80.

Joyner, U. T.; Horne, W. B.; and Leland, T. J. W. 1963. Investigations on the ground performance of aircraft relating to wet runway braking and slush drag. NASA, Langley Research Center, Hampton, Va. Paper presented to AGARD Flight Mechanics Panel, Paris, 14–18 Jan. 1963.

Kershner, William K. 1975. *The Flight Instructor's Manual.* Iowa State University Press, Ames.

Leland, T. J. W., and Taylor, G. R. 1964. *Effects of Tread Wear on the Wet Runway Braking Effectiveness of Aircraft Tires* RP-501. Langley Research Center, Hampton, Va.

Lowery, John. 1981. *Anatomy of a Spin.* Air Guide Publications, Long Beach, Calif.

McDonnell Douglas Corp. 1979. Fuel conservation DC9 series 20/30/40. *DC Flight Approach Magazine* 33.

Merritt, Leslie R. 1974. Impact of runway traction on possible approaches to certification and operation of jet transport aircraft 74-497. Society of Automotive Engineers.

Perkins, Courtland D., and Hage, Robert E. 1967. *Airplane Performance Stability and Control.* Wiley, New York.

Soderlind, Paul A. 1963. Jet turbulence penetration 8-63. Northwest Airlines. FSB

Sowa, Daniel F. 1974. Low level wind shear. *DC Flight Approach Magazine* 20.

Webb, Jim. 1971. *Fly the Wing.* Iowa State University Press, Ames.

INDEX